G000058977

£4.50

*Meditation: Its Process, Practice,
and Culmination*

Meditation: Its Process, Practice, and Culmination

by Swami Satprakashananda

(Author of *Methods of Knowledge, Hinduism and Christianity,
Sri Ramakrishna's Life and Message in the Present Age,*
and other Vedantic treatises)

THE VEDANTA SOCIETY OF ST. LOUIS

1976

Ramakrishna Vedanta Centre,
Unity House, Blind Lane,
Bourne End, Bucks. SL8 5LG.
Tel. No: Bourne End (06285) 26464

Copyright © 1976 by
The Vedanta Society of St. Louis
205 South Skinker Boulevard
St. Louis, Missouri 63105
All rights reserved.

Standard Book Number ISBN 0-916356-55-8
Library of Congress Catalog Card Number 76-15722

CONTENTS

PART TWO   Methods of Meditation

PART THREE   Appendices

ABBREVIATIONS

Ai.U.	*Aitareya Upanishad*
Ath.V.	*Atharva-Veda*
B.G.	*Bhagavad-gita*
Bh.S.	*Bhakti-sutras of Narada*
Br.Pu.	*Brahma Purana*
Br.U.	*Brihadaranyaka Upanishad*
B.S.	*Brahma-sutras*
Ch.U.	*Chhandogya Upanishad*
C.W.	*The Complete Works of Swami Vivekananda*
Dm.S.	*Dakshinamurti-stotra*
Gospel	*The Gospel of Sri Ramakrishna*
Great Master	*Sri Ramakrishna, the Great Master*
I.U.	*Isha Upanishad*
Ka.U.	*Katha Upanishad*
Ma.T.	*Mahanirvana Tantra*
Ma.U.	*Mandukya Upanishad*
Mu.U.	*Mundaka Upanishad*
NPT.U.	*Nrisinha-purva-tapaniya Upanishad*
Rg.V.	*Rig-Veda*
S.B.	*Srimad Bhagavatam*
Sd.	*Samkhya-darsanam*
Sk.	*Samkhya-karika*
S.V.	*Sama-Veda*
Sv.U.	*Svestasvatara Upanishad*
Sy.V.	*Sukla-yajur Veda*
Tai.Ar.	*Taittiriya Aranyaka*
Tai.U.	*Taittiriya Upanishad*
Vc.	*Viveka-chudamani*
Y.A.	*Yoga Aphorisms of Patanjali*

PREFACE

Meditation is the final spiritual course. Next to meditation is the realization of God, which is the goal of spiritual life. The practice of meditation cannot be efficacious until the mind definitely turns towards God. One has to go through certain preparatory courses in order to reach this stage. It is the steady observance of virtue and avoidance of vice that turns the human mind from the search of the temporal to the search of the eternal. Then comes the practice of Karma-yoga, which in due course leads to Bhakti-yoga and Jnana-yoga that prepare the ground for the practice of meditation.

In this book I have tried to delineate the various aspects of these spiritual courses from the beginning to the end.

I have also dwelt on the eight steps of Raja-yoga set forth by Patanjali, viz., 1) Yama, 2) Niyama, 3) Asana, 4) Pranayama, 5) Pratyahara, 6) Dharana, 7) Dhyana, 8) Samadhi. I have pointed out that these steps form the common background of man's entire spiritual life.

Vedanta accepts the practical courses of Patanjali, but not his dualistic philosophy.

The author.

PART ONE

Hymns and Prayers

(Translated by the author from the
Sanskrit originals)

Conducted Meditations

(Meditations conducted by the author
for the guidance of silent meditation
before his scriptural class)

A Vedic Prayer

In the beginning there was the Radiant Being,
   the Originator of the universe.
He became the Sole Ruler of all creation.
He upholds the earth, the heaven, and the
   inter-spaces,
To that Effulgent One we should offer worship.

He Who is the giver of spiritual knowledge and
   strength,
Whom the universe adores, Whose command
   the Gods obey,
Whose shade is immortality, Whose shadow is
   death,
To that Effulgent One we should offer worship.

He Who by His greatness has become the Supreme
   Lord of the living and the non-living,
Who governs all created beings,
To that Effulgent One we should offer worship.

He Who holds up the firmament, Who makes
   the sun stable, the earth and the heavenly
   bodies firm,
Who causes water to form in the sky,
To that Effulgent One we should offer worship.

(Rig-Veda X:121.1-3,5)

Hymn To Brahman

I

I bow to Thee, O Thou Pure Existence, the one Support
    of all the worlds;
I bow to Thee, O Thou Pure Intelligence, the one Self
    of the multiform universe;
I bow to Thee, the Nondual Being, the Giver of
    Freedom.
I bow to Thee, Supreme Brahman, Limitless and Absolute.

II

Thou art the sole Refuge; Thou alone art Adorable.
Thou alone art the Cause of the universe; Thou art
    in all beings.
Thou alone art the Creator, Ruler, and Destroyer
    of the universe.
Thou art the one undiversified, immutable Supreme Being.

III

The terror of terrors, the most terrible of the terrible;
The Goal of all beings, the purifier of all purifiers;
The highest of the high, the protector of all protectors;
Thou art the one Controller of the paramount powers.

IV

O the Supreme Lord, eternal, existent in all forms;
O Thou, the truth, indefinable, unattainable by the senses;
O Thou, the inconceivable, imperishable, all-pervasive
    Being;
O the Supreme Ruler, unmanifest, manifesting the
    universe, save us from misery.

V

On That alone we meditate, That alone we adore;
To that one Witness of the universe we bow down;
That one Existence, unsupported, supporting the universe;
The Ruler, the Abode, the boat to cross the ocean of
    life, is our sole refuge.

(Mahanirvana Tantra)

Eight Stanzas On Shukadeva[1]

I

Difference and non-difference having vanished in a trice,
    merits and demerits dissolved,
Where ignorance and delusion come to an end,
In him whose doubts are destroyed on attaining
    the knowledge of the Truth,
Beyond words, beyond the triad of the gunas;[2]
What direction, what prohibition for him who walks there
    on the path far above the gunas?

II

Seeing constantly the one Atman existing inside and
    outside all beings,
Like the one entire sky pervading everything,
Where remains no effect whatsoever different from
    the Cause;
What direction, what prohibition for him who walks there
    on the path far above the gunas?

[1]Shukadeva was a knower of Brahman, a living-free, illumined soul.
He was the son of the sage Vyasa, the author of the epic *Mahabharata* and
other classics. Shukadeva related to King Parikshit the *Bhagavatam* (The
Wisdom of God) composed by his father.

[2]The relative existence is composed of the three gunas (strands),
sattva, rajas, and *tamas. Sattva* is the principle of poise, conducive to
purity, knowledge, and joy. *Rajas* is the principle of motivity, leading to
activity, desire, and restlessness. *Tamas* is the principle of inertia,
resulting in inaction, dullness, and delusion.

III

Just as anything of gold becomes gold when put into fire,
As milk merges into milk, water into water, being
    of the same essence,
Similarly all "Thou's" dissolve into "That" in perfect
    oneness!
What direction, what prohibition for him who walks there
    on the path far above the gunas?

IV

Where the universe with all the worlds turns into one
    and the same essence,
Earth, water, fire, air, ether, and living beings,
    successively resolving into the Cause,
When salt waters lose themselves in the milk ocean
    of the Source;
What direction, what prohibition for him who walks there
    on the path far above the gunas?

V

Just as rivers and seas losing all differences become
    verily the ocean,
In the same way dissolve the living beings into
    One Existence-Knowledge-Bliss,
Beyond duality and distinction;
What direction, what prohibition for him who walks there
    on the path far above the gunas?

VI

Realizing the Supreme Being, the Goal of knowledge,
  as his very Self,
Seeing the One Self inside and outside all beings,
When he becomes Self-luminous, through the constant
  revelation of the Real;
What direction, what prohibition for him who walks there
  on the path far above the gunas?

VII

Just as a piece of burnt cloth exists only in appearance,
  even so is the life of him who is living-free,
Activity and inactivity being controlled by Nature,
  of neither is he the agent,
Freely he lives in the body, which he claims not;
What direction, what prohibition for him who walks there
  on the path far above the gunas?

VIII

Who am I here, or, art Thou? Where from? What for?
  Or what is this manifold here?
The Whole Truth, self-evident, becomes manifest like
  the sky,
Bliss is its name — partless, absolute Being, without
  beginning, middle, and end;
What direction, what prohibition for him who walks there
  on the path far above the gunas?

Hymn To The Divine Mother

Invocation

Come, O Divine Mother! Reveal Thyself unto us,
O the self-effulgent Deity!
O Thou, the Bestower of boons, the Revealer of
the Vedas, the Truth signified by the
three letters (Aum)!
O Thou, the Mother of metres, who art embodied
in the Gayatri prayer, who arisest from Brahman!
I bow to Thee.

Adoration

Be gracious, O Divine Mother! O Thou, the remover
of the distress of all who seek refuge in Thee!
Be gracious, O Thou, the Mother of the whole
universe!
O Thou, the Ruler of the universe, be gracious
and protect Thy creation.
Thou art the controller of the living and the
non-living.

O Thou of irresistible power! Thou art the sole
support of the world as the substance of earth.
Thou sustainest it as the substance of water.

Thou art the Divine Energy of infinite potency, the
Seed of the universe, the Supreme Maya.
All these beings are in delusion, O Divine Mother!
When Thou art gracious, Thou art the Way to
liberation.

All branches of knowledge are varied manifestations
of Thee.
All arts and all women in the world are Thy forms.
By Thee alone is everything pervaded, O Divine
Mother!
How can there be praise of Thee, who art beyond
praise, transcending the relative order, to which
the words belong.

Thou art all-in-all; Thou art the Giver of celestial
enjoyments and of Liberation.
When Thou art thus extolled, O Divine Mother, What
greater expression can there be for Thy praise?

Salutation

O Thou, who dwellest in the hearts of all
as intelligence!
O Thou, the Bestower of celestial enjoyments
and of Liberation!
I bow to Thee, O Divine Mother!

O Thou, who as the minute fractions of time,
    art the cause of all change!
O Thou, who art skillful in the dissolution
    of the universe!
I bow to Thee, O Divine Mother!

O Thou, the beneficence of all that are beneficent!
Thou art all good! In Thee is the fulfillment
    of all desires.
O Thou, the giver of refuge, the Three-eyed,
    the Radiant One!
I bow to Thee, O Divine Mother!

O Thou, the Divine Power of creation, preservation,
    and dissolution!
O Thou, the Eternal One, the support of the gunas,
    the embodiment of virtue!
I bow to Thee, O Divine Mother!

O Thou, who art ever ready to deliver the humble
    and the distressed that seek refuge in Thee!
O Thou, the remover of the sufferings of all!
I bow to Thee, O Divine Mother!

Hymn to the Divine Mother Durga[1]
The Destroyer Of Distress

I

Salutations to Thee, O Thou, the Sole Refuge of all,
   merciful and beneficent.
Salutations to Thee, O Thou, the Omnipresent One,
   manifest in all forms.
Salutations to Thee, O Thou, the Adorable of the world,
   with the blooming lotus feet.
Salutations to Thee, O Thou, the Savior of the World;
Save us, O Durga, the Destroyer of Distress!

II

Salutations to Thee, O Thou, the Eternal One, of whose
   existence the world is the proof.
Salutations to Thee, O Thou, the Mistress of Yoga, the
   Embodiment of Knowledge.
Salutations to Thee, O Thou, the Joy of the Ever-Blissful
   Supreme Being.
Salutations to Thee, O Thou, the Savior of the World;
Save us, O Durga, the Destroyer of Distress!

[1]Durga is the ten-handed Divine Mother, who holds a weapon in each hand to protect the ten directions of the universe. She is an embodiment of the Self-intelligent Divine Energy that governs relative existence.

III

Thou art the One Refuge, the Sole Deliverer of the
    destitute, the thirsty, the hungry, the distressed,
    the frightened, and the bound.
Salutations to Thee, O Thou, the Savior of the World;
Save us, O Durga, the Destroyer of Distress!

IV

In the horror of battlefield, in the stronghold of foes,
In forest, in fire, in the sea, in wilderness,
    in law courts,
Thou art the One Refuge, the Sole Protectress.
Salutations to Thee, O Thou, the Savior of the World;
Save us, O Durga, the Destroyer of Distress!

V

Thou art the One Refuge, the life-saving vessel of
    embodied beings drowning in the ocean of peril,
Boundless, tumultuous, dreadful, most difficult to
    cross.
Salutations to Thee, O Thou, the Savior of the world;
Save us, O Durga, the Destroyer of Distress!

VI

Salutations to Thee, O Thou, the Terror of Terrors,
Whose mighty hands with ease chased away the endless
    fears of the Chief of gods.
Thou art the One Refuge, the Remover of all obstacles,
Salutations to Thee, O Thou, the Savior of the World;
Save us, O Durga, the Destroyer of Distress!

VII

Thou art the One worshipped by Him Who has no rival!
Immeasurable, unconquered, true, furious, yet free
    from fury art Thou!
Thou dwellest in Ida, Pingala, and Susumna nerves!
Salutations to Thee, O Thou, the Savior of the World;
Save us, O Durga, the Destroyer of Distress!

VIII

Salutations to Thee, O Divine Durga, the Bestower of
    Good, even though terrifying.
Thou art the power of speech, Thou art Kundalini,
Thou art the inevitable fruit of action.
Thou art the manifestation, the darkness of dissolution,
    the truth, the guide.
Salutations to Thee, O Thou, the Savior of the World;
Save us, O Durga, the Destroyer of Distress!

IX

Thou art the Refuge of gods and demigods, of sages, of
    demons, and of men.
Of the afflicted, of the accused, of those surrounded
    by robbers Thou art the Sole Refuge.
Be gracious, O Divine Mother, the Destroyer of Distress.

(Vishvasara Tantra)

Evening Hymn To Sri Ramakrishna
Composed by Swami Vivekananda
(translated from the Bengali original)

I

I bow to Thee, O Thou, the breaker of the bond
   of birth and rebirth,
O Thou, the adoration of the world,
O Thou, the stainless one, the wearer of
   the human form,
Who art beyond the gunas, yet possessed of
   gunas [attributes].

II

O Thou, the remover of the contamination of sin,
O Thou, the adornment of the world, the embodiment
   of consciousness, whose eyes are purified by
   the collyrium of knowledge, at whose glance
   delusion disappears.

III

O Thou, the effulgent ocean of ecstasy, the
   ever-intoxicated boundless expanse of love,
   whose two feet attainable through devotion
   carry us across the ocean of life.

IV

O Thou, the God incarnate of the age, the Lord
of the universe; attended with the powers of
yoga, Thou hast Thy mind rapt and entranced,
I see Thee through Thy grace.

V

O Thou, the remover of the affliction of distress,
compassion personified; severe in work, Thou
hast given Thy life for the deliverance of
the world, and torn asunder the binding rope
of the Iron Age of Kali.

VI

Devoid of lust and greed, Thou hast strongly
censured sense-attachment.
O Thou, the Master-renouncer, O the Best of men,
grant us devotion to Thy feet.

VII

With Thy mind fearless, free from doubt and of
firm resolve,
Thou hast been the refuge of the devotees
without any condition, regardless of their
caste, family, or rank.

VIII

Thy venerable feet are the treasure which makes
the ocean of the world as easy to cross as
the foot-mark of a cow.
This Thou bestowest through love, O Thou of
equal sight, and the woes of the world vanish.

Evening Hymn To Sri Ramakrishna
(transliteration)

I

Khandana-bhava-bandhana jaga-bandana bandi tomaya

         3   4   1   2

Niranjana nara-rupa-dhara nirguna guna-maya

    5   6   7   8

(I) bow to Thee (O Thou), the breaker of the bond of birth and rebirth,

 1   2   3

(O Thou), the adoration of the world, (O Thou) the stainless One,

               4   5

the wearer of the human form, who art beyond the Gunas,

           6   7

(yet) possessed of gunas (attributes).

    8

II

Mochana-agha-dushana jaga-bhushana chid-ghana-kaya

       1   2   3

Jnananjana-bimala-nayana bikshane moha yaya

        4   5   6 7

(O Thou) the remover of the contamination of sin,(O Thou)

                   1

the adornment of the world, the embodiment of consciousness,

      2   3

whose eyes are purified by the collyrium of knowledge,

           4

at (whose) glance delusion disappears.

   5   6   7

3 *Chid-ghana-kaya* — lit. with the body *(kaya)* which is intelligence concretized *(ghana)*, or the embodiment of God-consciousness.
7 *yaya* — lit. departs, goes away.

III

Bhasvara bhava-sagara chira-unmada prema-pathar
   1   2   3   4

Bhaktyarjjana-yugala-charana tarana-bhava-para
        5   6

(O Thou), the effulgent ocean of ecstasy, the ever intoxicated
           1   2   3

boundless expanse of love, whose two feet attainable through devotion
      4   5

carry us across the ocean of life.
       6

5 *yugala* — pair, couple.
6 *tarana* — deliverer; *para* — shore.

IV

Jrimbhita-yuga-Ishvara jagadishvara yoga-sahaya
     1   2   3

Nirodhana-samahita-mana nirakhi tava kripaya
      4   5   6

(O Thou), the God incarnate of the age, the Lord of the universe,
          1   2

attended with (the powers of) yoga, Thou hast Thy mind rapt and
          3   4

entranced, (I) see (Thee) through Thy grace.
   4   5   6

1 *jrimbhita* — 'j' pronounced more like 'z'; lit., yawned; opened,
   manifested.
5 *nirakhi* — (I) see; (I see Thee as such): lit., discern, notice.
6 *tava* — Thy; *kripaya* — through grace.

V

Bhanjana-dukha-ganjana karuna-ghana karma-kathore
    1   2   3

pranarpana-jagata-tarana krintana-kalidore
          4   5

(O Thou), the remover of the affliction of distress, compassion personified;
                              1   2

severe in work, (Thou hast given Thy) life for the deliverance of the world,
        3   4

and torn asunder the binding rope of (the Iron Age of) Kali.
                              5

4 *pranarpana* — *prana* (life) *arpana* (giving, bestowal, whose life
has been given.

VI

Banchana-kama-kanchana atinindita-indriya-raga
        1   2

tyagishvara he naravara deha pade anuraga
    3   4   5   6   7   8

Devoid of lust and greed, (Thou) hast strongly censured sense-attachment,
              1   2

O Thou, the master-renouncer, O the Best of men, grant (us) devotion
              3   4   5   6   8

to (Thy) feet.
        7

2 *ati* — much; *nindita* — reproached; *indriya-raga* — sense-attachment.
3 *tyāgi* — renouncer. *Ishvara* — the Lord, the chief; lit., the ruler.

VII

Nirbhaya gata-samshaya dridha-nischaya manasa-van nishkarana
  1   2   3   4   5

bhakata-sharana tyaji jati-kula-mana
    6   7   8

With Thy mind fearless, free from doubt (and) of firm resolve, (Thou)
      4   1   2   3

hast been the refuge of the devotees without any condition, regardless of
              6   5   7

(their) caste, family, or rank.
             8

5 *nishkarana* — without cause(condition).
7 *tyaji* — lit., leaving, giving up; without considering.

VIII

Sampada tava shree-pada bhava-gospada-vari yathaya premarpana
    1   2   3   4   5   6

samadarashana jaga-jana-duhkha yaya
      7   8   9

Thy venerable feet (are) the treasure which makes the ocean of the world
 2   3   1   5   4

(as easy to cross as) the foot-mark of a cow. (This Thou) bestowest
           4   6

through love, (O Thou) of equal sight, (and) the woes of the world vanish.
    6   7   8   9

4 *bhava* — world; *gospada* — footmark of a cow; *vari* — water.
bhava-gospada-vari — (the ocean of) the world (becomes) as small as
water (accumulated in) the depression made by the hoof of a cow.
5 *yathaya* — at which, where.
6 *prema* — love; *arpana* — bestowal.
8 *jaga-jana* — men of the world *(jaga - jagat); duhkha* — sufferings.

Vedic Peace Chants

May my limbs, organ of speech, vital energy,
   eyes, ears, power, and all other senses
   fully develop.
The Whole universe is declared Brahman by
   the Upanishads.
May I never deny Brahman.
May Brahman never deny me.
May there be no denial from Him.
May there be no denial from me.
May the virtues as taught by the Upanishads
   dwell in me who am devoted to
   the Self [Brahman].
May the virtues dwell in me.

OM
Peace!　　　Peace!　　　Peace!

(Sama-Veda)

With our ears may we hear what is good,
   O Heavenly Beings!
With our eyes may we, the worshippers,
   see what is good.
With firm bodies and limbs may we, the
   adorers, live the life granted by the Deity.

OM
Peace!　　　Peace!　　　Peace!

(Atharva-Veda)

The Light Of Lights

We meditate on the sublime radiance
of the Effulgent Being,
the indwelling controller and sustainer
of all the worlds.
May He inspire our thought!

(Rg.V. 111:62.10)

Let us meditate on God so that we can realize Him. When we see God, all our fears and sufferings vanish, doubts and delusions dissolve, bondages shatter. We enter into the realm of Light where there is no trace of darkness, no shadow of death. We attain eternal life. We find ourselves free, illumined, and blissful. There is no way out of the miseries of life but through the direct vision of God.

He, the Supreme Consciousness, is the Light of all lights. It is He who manifests the universe. It is His Light that animates nature. The sun, the moon, the stars are but faint reflections of His supreme Light. He makes everything shine. Without His radiance the sun shines not, the moon is pale, the stars do not gleam, the lightning does not flash. He shining, everything shines. He makes everything real.

The self-effulgent Spirit, the Soul of the universe, is the Soul of all souls. Just as the same ocean exists at the back of each and every wave, so does He exist as the innermost Self of all. His Light endows the mind with intelligence and the eyes with sight. His Light enlivens the body and enables the mouth to speak, the ears to hear, the hands to work, the legs to move. His Light shines through each and every function of the mind and the senses. That Pure Consciousness has varied modes of expression, like the same transparent light shining differently through diverse mediums.

He is the Life of lives, the Ear of the ears, the Eye of the eyes. Through Him we live, through Him we move, through Him we see, through Him we act. It is He who makes all actions and perceptions possible. Within us and around us He alone shines.

But though living and moving in Him, we know Him not. Like blind men wandering about in the full blaze of the mid-day sun we are unaware of Him. The moment the scales of darkness fall from our eyes, we see Him shining in full glory in and through all things and beings.

> With hands and feet everywhere,
> with eyes, heads, and mouths everywhere,
> with ears everywhere in the universe —
> That exists, pervading all.
>
> (B.G. XIII:13)

The more we think of Him, the more we open our minds to Him, the clearer grows our vision of Him. Let us meditate on Him intently with devotion until we feel suffused with His Light, animated by His Spirit, and directed by His Presence, until He reveals Himself unto us and we see Him shining in and through us as the one effulgent ocean of Bliss.

As the innermost self within us, He is the nearest of the near. Visualize Him in the depth of your heart as the Light of all lights, shining with constant effulgence.

In the precious golden case of inner consciousness is the Supreme Brahman, ever pure and
partless, the all-white Light of lights.
Hence, the knowers of the Self know That.

(Mu.U. II:2.9)

Om, Shanti, Shanti, Shanti.
Peace, Peace, Peace unto all.

Him We Worship

Thou art power, give us power.
Thou art strength, give us strength.
Thou art energy, give us energy.
Thou art vigour, give us vigour.
Thou art wrath [against wrong],
give us wrath.
Thou art tolerance, give us tolerance.

(Sy.V. XIX:9)

God is the one source of all power, all strength, all
energy, all vitality — physical, mental, moral, and spiritual.
All greatness is His greatness, all glory His glory, all
goodness His goodness. He is the life of the living, the
sentiency of the sentient. It is His light that illumines the
mind and enriches the heart.

Says Sri Krishna,

Whatever being is powerful, beautiful, or glorious,
know thou that to have sprung from a fraction of My
effulgence.

I exist sustaining the whole world by a portion of Myself.

(B.G. X:41,42)

The glory of the rising sun, the splendour of the starry
firmament, the sublimity of the snow-capped mountain
ranges, the majesty of the boundless rolling waters are but
faint reflections of His radiance.

At His command the wind blows, the sun shines, fire
burns, rain falls.

Under the mighty rule of this Immutable, O Gargi,[1]
the sun and the moon are held in their places;
under the mighty rule of this Immutable, O Gargi,
heaven and earth maintain their positions;
under the mighty rule of this Immutable, O Gargi,
moments, hours, days and nights, fortnights and months,
seasons and years are held in their respective places.
Under the mighty rule of this Immutable, O Gargi,
some rivers flow eastward from the white mountains,
others, flowing westward, continue in that direction,
and still others keep to their respective courses . . .

Whosoever, O Gargi, departs from this world without
knowing this Immutable is miserable.
But He, O Gargi, who departs from this world after
knowing this Immutable is a knower of Brahman (the
Supreme Being).

. . . There is no other witness but This, no other hearer
but This, no other thinker but This, no other knower but
This.

(Br.U. III:8.9-11)

The almighty, all-knowing Lord is at the same time all-
merciful, all-loving, all-beautiful, all-blissful. It is His
beauty that makes nature beautiful. It is His love that makes
men loving; it is His joy that makes them joyous. He is ever-
ready to help us. We can have whatever we want from Him
just for the asking. If we pray to Him for earthly possessions,
power, honor and fame, we shall get them from Him. But
they are perishable and infected by pain; we have to leave
them at death.

---

[1]The sage Yajnavalkya answers the questions of Gargi, a woman
philosopher.

If we pray to Him for heavenly enjoyments, He will grant them to us also. But these, too, are impermanent and compare not with the eternal divine treasures.

> There is no happiness in the finite. The infinite alone is happiness; the infinite alone should be known.
>
> (Ch.U. VI:23)

Let us pray to Him for Divine Knowledge, Divine Love, Divine Life, Divine Bliss. Who but a fool will beg trinkets of the Emperor of emperors, the Maker, the Ruler of the universe? Who but a fool will collect glass beads after finding an immense diamond mine? Who but a fool will allay his thirst with ditch-water when he sees the perennial fountain of ambrosia ahead?

As long as the ego prevails in us, as long as we hold ourselves separate from God, we cannot outgrow our limitations, no matter where we go, what we do, whatever we attain. When we seek God for God's sake and find Him and become united with Him, then only do we become heirs to Divine Wisdom, Freedom, Love and Joy in the true sense. Let us seek Him and Him alone; love Him and Him alone; worship Him and Him alone.

For this we need strength — physical, mental, moral and spiritual. It is through His power that we can walk in His path. It is through His light that we can find Him. It is through His grace that we can adore Him. It is through His love that we can be united with Him. He is,

> the Goal, the Protector, the Master, the Witness, the Abode, the Refuge, the Friend.
>
> (B.G. IX:18)

He, who is the giver of Self-knowledge and strength,
Whom the universe adores,
Whose command the cosmic forces obey,
Whose shelter is immortality,
Whose shadow is death —
to that Self-effulgent Being we offer our worship.

(Rg.V. X:121.3)

Whatever power we hold, whatever knowledge we possess, whatever joy we find in life, all derive from Him. Yet we cannot have any of these in their intrinsic purity nor in adequate measure, simply because we do not feel our essential unity with the Lord, the Soul of all souls. Our ego intervenes, creates a barrier, as it were, and obstructs the course.

Think that you are ever united with Him, that He is the sole Master and you are a mere instrument, that you belong to Him completely as a drop of water belongs to the ocean, that all you have to do is to seek Him, to worship Him, to surrender yourself to Him. Think that Divine Knowledge, Divine Purity, Divine Bliss are seeking a channel of expression in you and will flow into you the moment you are ready. Think that like the water-jar immersed in the sea, you are in Him, and He is in you.

That Self-effulgent Being who is in fire, in
water, in herbs, in trees, who pervades the whole
universe, to that ever-shining Lord we bow down
again and again.

(Sv.U. II:17)

Om, Shanti, Shanti, Shanti.
Peace, Peace, Peace unto all.

Peace That Passeth Understanding

> There is peace in heaven, peace in the sky,
> peace on earth, peace in waters, peace in herbs,
> peace in trees, peace in the deities, peace in
> Brahman, peace in all, peace in peace.
> May that peace be unto me.
>
> (Sy.V. XXXVI:17)

An ineffable peace dwells in the heart of the universe. This is its very essence. It permeates everything. All beings and things rest on the same Being which is Bliss itself. Essentially it is one existence, undivided, undiversified, immovable, no matter what differences, divisions, movements and discords may appear to us in the phenomenal world.

The one immutable Being holds everything. The forms change, but not the substance. Men, animals, trees and mountains, the sun, the moon, the stars and all beings are knit together, as it were, by a single golden cord permeating them. Says Sri Krishna,

> Beyond Me there is nothing else. All this is strung in Me
> as a row of gems on a thread.
>
> (B.G. VII:7)

In Him we live, in Him we move, and in Him we have our being. As we think of the Divine Spirit as the one Self of all, we perceive our unity with all things and beings. We feel we belong to the Infinite Being and through Him to all, and not to a particular family, society and country, race, nation and so forth. Nothing seems to be alien, strange, or remote, but everything near and akin. All prejudice and antipathy leave the mind. Peace and love dwell within us.

> He who is the Real among the unreal, who is the Omniscient among the sentient, who, though One, dispenses desired objects to many (according to their actions), those wise persons who realize that indwelling Being, to them belongs eternal peace and not to others.
> (Ka.U. V:13)

Contemplate your relationship with all through the all-pervading divine Self. Think that you are at peace with everyone and everyone is at peace with you, that you fear no one and no one fears you. Think that the atmosphere around you is peaceful; the air you breathe is pure and wholesome. Think that as you inhale the air it purifies you through and through. You have a pure body and a pure mind. Purity brings calmness. Your body has become steady and poised and the mind quiet.

Turn your inner eye on the mind and watch it. Visualize the mind as a lake with a placid surface, free from all ripples, bubbles and eddies. Look through its crystal pure water into the depth of your being and envisage the innermost Self, pure, free, shining and blissful. As you view the Self you become one with it. You go beyond the mind. You find yourself ever distinct from it as its witness. No longer do you identify yourself with the body or the mind. You become detached from both.

Physical and mental conditions, hunger and thirst,

growth and decay, pain and pleasure, hope and fear cannot affect you any more. Neither the body or the mind can limit you. Beyond them both you find yourself in the limitless, changeless, ever-free, ever-calm Divine Being. You attain eternal peace, the peace of God that passeth all understanding.

> When the seer sees the Radiant Being, the Maker, the Ruler, the Origin of origins, then he, having shaken off merits and demerits, stainless and illumined, attains supreme calmness.
>
> (Mu.U. III:1.3)

Om, Shanti, Shanti, Shanti.
Peace, Peace, Peace unto all.

The Source Of All Delight

> From Bliss all these beings arise,
> by Bliss they live, into Bliss they
> go and re-enter.
>
> (Tai. U. III:6)

There is Bliss in the heart of each and everything. Bliss is the very essence of the universe.

That Supreme Bliss is so pure and transcendental that no commotion, conflict, or catastrophe can touch It. The tumult and turmoil of the world cannot reach It. No misery, pain or fear can mingle with It. All these appear and disappear like froth and bubbles in the profound ocean of Bliss.

We cannot perceive that Bliss in its essential purity because of the impurities and distractions of the mind. The faintest perception of this Bliss fills your heart with peace and joy whenever and wherever the mind is calm. As the sunlight revealing various objects — dark or white, large or small, high or low, good or bad — does not lose its native transparency, just so the Supreme Bliss, pervading everything, prevailing everywhere, ever retains Its innate purity.

Pure Bliss is the very substance of the universe, the Reality itself. The Real is all-bliss, being unconditioned, free, pure and perfect. The Real is Self-aware, real unto Itself. So Bliss is identical with Absolute Consciousness, Awareness Itself.

Bliss is Brahman.   (Tai.U. III:6)

An infinitesimal part of that Bliss being manifest in this universe has made it blissful.

On a minute fraction of that Bliss other beings live.
(Br.U. IV:3.32)

Who can exhale or inhale if this Bliss did not dwell in the depth of the heart?   (Tai.U. II:7)

Think that Bliss pervades the atmosphere around you, that the air you breathe is pure, sweet, and serene. Think that your entire being — body, mind, the organs and the senses — are permeated by that Bliss. You feel soothed and refreshed. Your body is poised; your mind is calm. You experience an ineffable peace and joy arising from within.

Pure Bliss is manifest within us as the very Self. So the Self is the dearest of all. We love everything else for the sake of the Self. The Self being reflected in the body, makes the body dear.

O my beloved,[1] it is not for the sake of the husband that the husband is dear, but for the sake of the Self the husband is dear. Not for the sake of the sons are the sons dear, but for the sake of the Self the sons are dear. Not for the sake of wealth is wealth dear, but for the sake of the Self wealth is dear. Not for the sake of the animals are the animals dear, but for the sake of the Self the animals are dear. It is not for the sake of anything that anything is dear, but for the sake of the Self that everything is dear.

O Maitreyi, the Self should be realized, should be heard, reflected on and meditated upon.

(Br.U. IV:5.6)

[1]The sage Yajnavalkya addresses his wife, Maitreyi.

The Self is the source of all delight. Our happiness does not originate, as we think, from the mental states or the sense objects, or the contact of the senses with the objects. Whatever joy we seem to get from sense experience, thoughts, feelings, memories, actually derives from the Self, and not from any of these processes. Whenever the mind is steadied by any of these the native joy of the Self flows into it. We do not perceive joy in its intrinsic purity because it gets coloured in the process of permeation.

Dive deep within yourself into that inexhaustible source of all blessedness. It is the endless ocean of joy abounding in treasures. As you enter into it you gain pearls of devotion, wisdom, purity, love and peace in abundance. Imagine that you are fully immersed in it. Above you, below you, around you there are but the waters of immortal Bliss. You feel free as a fish in the sea. There is no fear of death in this ocean. If you lose yourself in it, you find yourself, you become what you really are; you attain self-fulfillment.

> Verily, Brahman is Bliss. It is by attaining Bliss, that the knowers of Brahman become blessed.
> One who experiences the Bliss of Brahman beyond words and thoughts has nothing to fear.
> (Tai.U. II:7,9)

> May I attain Brahman. May I attain Supreme Bliss. May I attain Brahman, who is Supreme Bliss!
> (Tai.Ar. X:39)

Om, Shanti, Shanti, Shanti.
Peace, Peace, Peace unto all.

Right Understanding

May He, the Lord of the Universe, the Great
Seer, the Terror of evil, the Originator and Sustainer of heavenly beings, who created the
cosmic being in the beginning, endow us with
salutary understanding.   (Sv.U. III:4)

May the effulgent Supreme Being, who,
though one and undiversified and self-fulfilled,
creates innumerable forms in the beginning by
His manifold powers and reabsorbs the universe
at the end, endow us with salutary understanding.
(Sv.U. IV:11)

An essential requisite in life is right understanding. We
need this inner light to see the way in all circumstances. In
this world of duality, good and evil, right and wrong, truth
and falsehood are so intermixed that a clear understanding
is indispensable for a right choice at each and every step of
life. Through it we can view things in the true perspective
and appraise them correctly. It enables us to distinguish
between the good and the pleasant, the essential and the
non-essential, the primary and the secondary, the Real and
the unreal. Thus it prevents confusion and infuses
conviction in us. With this inner eye open, we feel we walk in
light.

A person may have wealth and position without being
able to use them judiciously for lack of right understanding;
rather there is every chance of his losing them by unwise
measures. On the other hand, a man having no rank or

power can rise to the heights of glory by the exercise of right understanding. Even when all external resources fail, the right understanding alone can guide us out of all difficulties and dangers. It teaches us how to make necessary adjustments in all conditions. It exhorts us to be at our best in each and every situation. There is no obstacle which cannot be overcome, no problem which cannot be solved, no plight from which there is no escape, when we can read the situation aright with a clear understanding and a well-balanced mind.

Right understanding develops when the mind is purified. It is the same as pure intellect. It does not function unless the mind is calm. Mental purity and calmness go together. Moral impurity blurs our vision and prevents us from seeing things in their true light. Even if by some means we come to know the right course, we are not able to pursue it as long as the wrong tendencies prevail in us. As it often happens, emotions like anger, pride, greed, jealousy, hatred, fear and lust unbalance the mind, overpower will and hoodwink reason.

So when we pray to God for right understanding, we should at the same time try our utmost to be pure in thought, speech and deed, and pray to Him to help us be so. Prayers are readily responded to only when we are sincere, when we make the best use of our existing capacities howsoever limited they may be. Whatever resources God has already provided us with we must utilize fully before we ask for more. "Heaven helps those that help themselves" is not a saying without meaning.

We have to pray to God. With all our weaknesses, how can we depend solely on ourselves? Try howsoever we may, self-effort alone proves inadequate for our upliftment. Can the bound free themselves? Can the blind be their own guides? After continuous struggle and repeated failures we realize more than ever how weak we are, how strong is our attachment to sense-life, how deep-seated are the passions and propensities in us. To eradicate them seems to be beyond mortal power. Then we feel the absolute need of divine help, guidance and grace. Then we pray to God with all sincerity and humility.

We surrender ourselves to Him, yet our efforts do not cease. We struggle, depending on His grace for success. Who but the all-loving, all-merciful Maker and Ruler of the universe can forgive our faults, make us free from all sins and vices, and lead us in His path amidst the allurements of life? Who but the all-seeing Supreme Being can endow us with the inner vision to see the Light in this world of darkness and delusion? Who but the ever-free, ever-pure omnipotent Lord can remove all our bondages, miseries and delusions and make us eternally free, pure, and perfect?

Right understanding is a rare gift of God. As it develops, the light of Truth dawns upon us. We learn to discriminate between the eternal and the evanescent, the real and the unreal, the relative and the absolute. Eventually we know God alone is real; He alone exists in the true sense. It is His reality that makes everything real. He who is pure Existence-Knowledge-Bliss is the one substance of all changing forms, the one all-pervasive Self of the manifold universe. In him alone is true life, true light, true peace, true freedom.

With true understanding we seek God and God alone. We pray to Him, we worship Him, not for material treasures and joys, here or hereafter, but for divine love and wisdom. We crave His direct vision. We love Him alone. Whatever else we love, we love for Him and through Him. Our entire life centers in Him. We think about Him, we talk about Him, we work for Him, we live for Him.

Of such devotees of God, Sri Krishna speaks thus:

> With their minds wholly in Me, with their life absorbed in Me, enlightening one another and always speaking of Me, they obtain satisfaction and delight.
>
> To them, ever devout and worshipping Me with love, I give the spiritual insight by which they come to Me.
>
> Out of mere compassion for them, I, abiding in their hearts, by the shining lamp of knowledge destroy the darkness born of ignorance.
>
> (B.G. X:9-11)

The "shining lamp of knowledge" which removes all ignorance and reveals God, is the spiritual intuition into which the right understanding bestowed upon us by Him develops through His grace. Shankaracharya gives a graphic description of this lamp of knowledge in his commentary on the passage quoted above.

> The lamp of knowledge characterized by dis-criminatory intellect, fed by the oil of pure devotion, fanned by the air of absorbing thoughts on Me, furnished with the wick of insight, evolved by the cultivation of continence and other virtues, held in the receptacle of the heart free from worldliness, placed in the wind-sheltered enclosure of the mind withdrawn from sense-objects and untainted by attachment and aversion, shining with the light of right knowledge produced by the incessant practice of earnest meditation.

Think that a ray of the Divine Sun shining in the spiritual firmament has entered into your heart in the form of right understanding and lighted the "shining lamp of knowledge," which is removing all darkness and delusions from within you and revealing Him as the all-pervasive light of pure Consciousness. Meditate on this ocean of effulgent Bliss existing within you, around you, above you, below you and permeating you through and through, until you feel you are one with That.

> That vast self-luminous inconceivable Being, subtler than the subtle, shines in various forms. That is farther than the farthest and also near, here. To the seers That is seated right here in the depths of their heart.
>
> He is not grasped by the eye, nor by speech, nor by other senses, nor by austerities, nor by work. But he whose mind is purified by the clearness of knowledge sees Him, the Absolute, through meditation.
>
> (Mu.U. III:1.7,8)
>
> May we realize Brahman by right understanding. May we realize Supreme Bliss by right understanding. May we realize Brahman, Who is Supreme Bliss, by right understanding.
>
> (Tai.Ar. X:39)

Om, Shanti, Shanti, Shanti.
Peace, Peace, Peace unto all.

Not By Thy Law But By Thy Grace

> Unborn that Thou art,
> I as one afraid of birth and death,
> seek refuge in Thee.
> O Thou the Terrible One!
> Ever protect me by Thy benign face.
>
> (Sv.U. IV:21)

Not by Thy law but by Thy grace can I be saved. Thou alone art immortal in this mortal universe. Thou alone art eternal in the midst of the evanescent. Thou art the one immutable Being underlying all transitory forms. Finite things and beings pass away. But Thou abidest forever. Beyond birth, beyond death, beyond growth, beyond decay art Thou. Everything begins in time and ends in time. But time begins and ends in Thee. Timeless art Thou, without beginning and without end.

In this world of ceaseless change Thou art my sole refuge. On none else can I rely; nothing else can I hold to in this life. Youth, beauty, power and prosperity come and go. Friends come and go. Nothing is constant. Pain and pleasure, growth and decay, triumph and defeat, birth and death are my inevitable lot in this mortal plane. There is no security anywhere but in Thee. None but Thou canst save me from bondages, sufferings, delusions and death.

Thou art the sole reality in all that appears to be real. Everything exists because of Thee. Behind the shifting scenes of life and death, of light and darkness, of creation and destruction, of rise and fall, of harmony and discord, Thou shinest forever. Unobserved, Thou observest everything; unseen, Thou seest everything; unheard, Thou hearest everything. Unknown, Thou knowest everything; unsupported, Thou supportest everything, unchanging, Thou holdest all that changes. From Thee the universe arises, by Thee it is sustained, into Thee it is reabsorbed. Throughout the projection, preservation and dissolution of the universe Thou art ever awake.

Thou art the stern Ruler of the universe. Thy laws govern nature. At Thy command the sun shines, the planets keep to their respective courses, the seasons change. At Thy command wind blows and fire burns. With unerring justice Thou dispensest to human beings the fruits of their good and evil deeds. As they sow, so they reap. None can escape Thy inexorable law.

What can save me then? Bound by desires, over-powered by weaknesses, thwarted by evil tendencies born of past karma, I find no strength to rescue myself. I try to practice virtue, but I fail. Even when I know the right course, I cannot follow it. My emotions, thoughts and actions are not under my control. I am weak. How can I stand on my own feet? I am blinded by ignorance. How can I find my way? I am bound. How can I free myself? Therefore, O Lord, I have no other way to Liberation but through Thy grace. I surrender myself to Thee. Not by Thy law, but by Thy grace can I be saved. Be gracious unto me.

I do not know how to pray to Thee. I do not know how to worship Thee. I do not know how to meditate on Thee. I have no merit whatsoever. I depend wholly on Thy mercy. I take refuge in Thee. Thy grace is my only support, my only treasure, my only equipment in the journey through life. Be gracious unto me!

Thou art severe and Thou art beneficent. Thou art the subduer of the wicked and Thou art the protector of the virtuous. Thou art the dispenser of justice and Thou art the bestower of mercy. Thou art the stern Ruler and Thou art the compassionate Father. In destruction as well as in creation Thy benign hand works. In prosperity and adversity, in beauty and ugliness, Thy will prevails. Thou art terrible and Thou art blissful.

> With hands and feet everywhere, with eyes, heads and mouths everywhere, with ears everywhere, That exists pervading everything in the universe.
>
> The wise realize Him as shining through the functions of all the senses, yet without the senses, as the Lord of all, the Ruler of all, the Refuge and the Friend of all.
>
> (Sv.U. III:16,17)

Think that though you do not see God, He is constantly watching you and protecting you. He is ever ready to help you, guide you, and reveal Himself unto you. But you pay no attention to Him. You can get whatever you want just for the asking. "Ask, and it shall be given you,"[1] says Jesus Christ. Pray to Him to reveal Himself unto you.

Imagine that you are in the very presence of the Divine Lord. You see His blissful form, radiant with joy, beauty, wisdom and love. You see His benign face with soul-enthralling smile. You see His compassionate eyes showering grace upon you. You prostrate yourself at His feet.

[1] St. Matthew 7:7.

Lo! The Lord in His infinite kindness and unbounded love takes you up in His loving arms. You feel that you are a child reposing in the bosom of the Divine Father. You feel that you are within Him, you are one with Him. Around you, above you, within you, He alone exists.

He is the Life of your life, the Soul of your soul. He fills you through and through. You are suffused by Divine Radiance. Your egoism vanishes, leaving just a shadow. You realize yourself as a channel for the expression of divine power, divine wisdom, divine love. He sees through your eyes. He hears through your ears. He speaks through your mouth. He works through your hands. In fact, it is all He, not you. Those eyes are His eyes, those ears are His ears, those hands His hands, those lips His lips. You are His; He is yours.

I bow to Brahman, the Supreme Being, Who is All-Bliss, Who is present everywhere, Who was in the past, Who will be in the future.

(Ath.V. X:8.1)

I know that Immutable, Eternal Being, Who is the Self of all, Who is omnipresent because of His all-pervasiveness, Whom the knowers of Brahman declare as birthless and perfect.

(Sv.U. III:21)

Om, Shanti, Shanti, Shanti.
Peace, Peace, Peace unto all.

He Is The Goal, He Is The Way

> Purified by the all-holy, omnipresent, eternal
> Being, man gets rid of the evil effects of his mis-
> deeds. Purified by the same ever-pure Divine
> Being, we can overcome deadly sin, our enemy!
> (Tai.Ar. X:11)

God is all-holy. He is Pure Spirit free from all taint of matter. He is the very Light of Consciousness, ever-shining, self-luminous. There is no trace of darkness in Him. On the contrary, He is the remover of all darkness. He illuminates everything. Without Him nothing can shine, neither the sun, nor moon, nor fire. All knowledge is a reflection of His light.

Impurity dwells in darkness, in ignorance. He, the Light of all lights, is absolutely pure, spotless. The Upanishads declare Him as "blameless, stainless, all white without blemish."[1] He is purity itself. None can be pure but through Him. He is the sole purifier. By His light alone we can be free from all impurities, weaknesses and bondages.

Being devoid of Divine Light, we are veiled by ignorance, which is the root of all wrong thoughts and actions. From ignorance stems egoism. Being unaware of the true self, the immortal spirit within us, and its unity with the Supreme Spirit, we identify ourselves with the physical and psychophysical system and behave, to all appearances,

[1] Sv.U. VI:19; I.U. 8.

as distinct individuals separate from and independent of the Divinity. From egoism proceeds likes and dislikes, attachment and aversion. It creates in us sense desires, selfishness, pride and delusion, and prepares the ground for other vices.

In order to get rid of all evil, we must therefore be free from egoism. We shall not have to discard the ego, the individual self; we have to attune it to the Supreme Spirit, we must feel our essential unity with Him.

The individual will must be submitted to the Divine Will. The Lord is the Operator, we are mere instruments. He is the sole Master, we are mere servants. Everything belongs to Him and Him alone. All power is His power, all knowledge His knowledge, all beauty His beauty, all greatness His greatness. Therefore all sense of separateness and all idea of independence from the Divinity have to be given up.

We must realize that as drops of water to the ocean, as rays of light to the sun, as sparks of flame to the fire, we are ever related to Him; we do not perceive the unity simply because of ignorance. Thus we must loosen the grip of egoism. Then divine power, divine light, divine life will flow into us, unobstructed, unstained. We shall be the right channels for their expression.

When egoism recedes, God's grace descends upon us. God takes care of us as soon as we depend upon Him. He guides us when we resign ourselves to His guidance. His light shines within us and chases away all darkness, all impurities, when we open our hearts to it. Virtuous or sinful, anyone can receive His grace simply by self-surrender. Through His mercy a sinner can be a saint in no time.

Declares Sri Krishna,

> Even the most sinful man, if he worships Me with unswerving devotion, must be regarded as righteous, for he has formed the right resolution. Soon he becomes righteous and attains eternal peace. Do thou proclaim it, O son of Kunti, that My devotee never perishes.
>
> (B.G. IX:30,31)

Mere righteousness without devotion to God cannot liberate us from the bondage of duality such as birth and death, pain and pleasure, light and darkness, rise and fall. As long as egoism persists, as long as an individual holds to "I-ness" and "my-ness" and arrogates to himself any power, any knowledge, any work and its result, all his good actions as well as evil will bind him to the relative existence — the good like a golden chain, the evil like an iron chain, but both equally strong to bind.

If good deeds prevail in his life he will be led after death to an agreeable state of existence, either on this earth or elsewhere. But every situation in the relative plane must be fraught with fear; however exalted, however prosperous, however pleasant it may be, it cannot be an unmixed blessing. Just as there is bitterness in want, so there is bitterness in plenty. Just as adversity is a problem, so is prosperity. Just as pain has a sting, so has pleasure.

Even the joys and glories of Paradise attainable by virtuous deeds have their limitations and come to an end, being produced by finite work. They cannot satisfy man's innermost longing for the Ultimate, the Supreme. They pale into insignificance compared with the absolute freedom and blissfulness of the Self that man can realize through the recognition of his essential unity with the Divinity.

When a person resigns himself to God's care, God leads him out of the maze of relative existence unto Himself. It is through His light, through His guidance, through His grace that we can go beyond the wilderness of life and reach Him. Sri Krishna declares,

> But those who consecrate all their actions to Me, regard Me as the Supreme Goal and worship Me, meditating on Me with single-minded devotion, to them whose minds are fixed on Me, I become ere long, O Son of Pritha, the deliverer out of the ocean of mortal existence.
>
> (B.G. XII:6,7)

Think that as you turn your mind to God, as you surrender yourself to Him, His light shines inside your heart. It chases away all darkness, all dross and dirt from within. It rectifies all the twists and turns of the mind.

You see the mind, smooth and clean, shining like a mirror. The Divine Light is reflected on it. This is the light of Supreme Bliss, of Infinite Knowledge and of Eternal Life. Your whole being is vibrant with ineffable joy. As you meditate on Him more and more deeply, the mirror of the mind becomes as transparent as the purest crystal. The Divine Consciousness radiates distinctly, clearly, through the pristine purity of the mind.

Gradually the mind, suffused with the light of the Spirit, dissolves and the Divine Being becomes fully manifest. You attain the direct and immediate awareness of Godhead. Your ego becomes completely merged in Him, and the one Infinite, Eternal Being, beyond all duality, beyond all difference and distinction, shines in your consciousness.

I bow to God, the destroyer of the round of birth and rebirth, the giver of liberation,

Who is the Supreme Lord, immutable and all-pervasive, beyond the manifest and the unmanifest, free from manifoldness, ever-blissful, ever-gracious, ever-pure, attributeless, stainless, limitless like the sky,

Whom the wise meditate upon in Samadhi.

(Br.Pu. Ch.I)

Om, Shanti, Shanti, Shanti.
Peace, Peace, Peace unto all.

He Makes All Things Dear

May the winds blow sweetly.
May the rivers flow sweetly.
May the plants yield sweet crops to us.
May night and day bring us sweetness.
May the dust of the earth be filled with sweetness.
May the heavens protect us with sweet rain.
May the trees bear sweet fruits to us.
May the sun shine sweetly upon us.
May there be sweetness in all directions.

(Rg.V. I:90.6-8)

An ineffable Bliss pervades the universe. This is its very essence. Verily, from Bliss all beings arise. By Bliss they are sustained. Into Bliss they move and re-enter.

Supreme Bliss is identical with Supreme Consciousness. The Omnipresent Being, the Self of the universe, is an effulgent ocean of Bliss. Though all-pervading, He is transcendentally pure and unrelated, so that no excitement, no discord, no evil whatsoever of the phenomenal world can contaminate Him. Just as a colorless, clear crystal appearing red in association with something red is not tainted by redness, similarly the Supreme Self is untarnished by the world-appearance. Being unattached He is unaffected. Ever free, pure, stainless, blameless is He.

We live and move in that effulgent ocean of Bliss. Yet we are unaware of this fact, simply because our minds are not receptive, simply because our inner vision is obscured by delusion. We can experience ineffable joy anywhere at any time, if our minds be pure and calm.

That effulgent Bliss, permeating everything, is manifest within each individual being as the innermost self. This is why the self is ever dear to him. Whatever else is dear to him is dear through the self. Because of its association with the spiritual self, the body is dear. Because of its association with the spiritual self through the body, the family is dear. Just as every wave of the ocean is essentially one with the entire mass of water, so is the individual self essentially one with the Supreme Self.

Being an effulgent ocean of Bliss, the Supreme Self is the dearest of all. Everything is dear for His sake. The husband is dear, not for the sake of the husband, but for the sake of the Self. The wife is dear, not for the sake of the wife, but for the sake of the Self. The children are dear, not for the sake of the children, but for the sake of the Self. Wealth is dear, not for the sake of wealth, but for the sake of the Self.

On a particle of His Bliss all creatures live. He is the one source of all joy. It is by attaining that Bliss that one becomes joyous. Who could inhale, who could exhale, if the blissful self did not dwell within?

Whatever joy a person experiences arises from the blissful self through the modes of the mind. As long as he is unaware of the true nature of the self, he cannot experience joy in its native purity. It is the mental modes through which joy flows or trickles that create all differences in its character and degree. The external objects do not produce happiness. At best they induce internal states more or less favorable to the flow of joy from the self. Even without any external stimulus there can be the internal condition conducive to the experience of joy.

The blissfulness of the self has varied expressions as sense pleasure, as intellectual satisfaction, as aesthetic felicity, as moral delight, and as spiritual beautitude according to the condition of the mind. Essentially, there is no difference between one kind and another. But the difference in the mediums of expression produces different results, even as water flowing through different channels produces different effects on life.

Intellectual pleasure is higher than sense pleasure, because man's rational nature, being superior to his physical nature, serves as a better medium for the expression of the joyousness of the self. Similarly, moral delight is purer and deeper than intellectual delight, because man's moral nature, being higher than his rational nature, serves as a better medium for the expression of the joyousness of the self. But the spiritual joy surpasses all other joys, for man's spiritual nature, which is also a state of the mind, is closest to the blissful self.

Underlying the varying states of the mind and the body, the blissful self shines in pristine glory, unaffected by virtue and vice, hope and fear, pain and pleasure, knowledge and ignorance, hunger and thirst, health and sickness. This is man's true being, ever pure, free and blessed.

But being identified with the psychophysical system through mysterious ignorance he does not realize himself as such. Deep meditation on the real nature of the self counteracts this ignorance. Then the self freed from the grip of egoism shines in full glory. Untrammeled by physical and psychical conditions the individual self realizes its essential oneness with the Supreme Self and enters into absolute peace and blessedness.

Think that you are pure and blissful, that you are of the same essence as the Supreme Being, that you are of the nature of effulgent Bliss that He is. Visualize the spiritual self as the most precious jewel, emitting pure and serene rays of bliss soothing the body and the mind. Meditate on this intensely as your very being.

As you identify yourself with this, ignorance vanishes. While visualizing the blissful self you dive deep into the boundless ocean of effulgent Bliss. "There is no joy in the finite, the Infinite alone is joy." "He is below, He is above, He is behind, He is before. He is in the south, He is in the north, He is all these." He shines through all forms. To a knower of Brahman everything is permeated by effulgent Bliss. May everything be favorable to us, as we seek Brahman, who is all-bliss.

> May the world become peaceful. May all men and women be gentle and honest. May all think of mutual welfare. May the minds of all be turned to the highest good. May there be devotion in the hearts of all to the Supreme Lord.
> (S.B. V:18.9)

Om, Shanti, Shanti, Shanti.
Peace, Peace, Peace unto all.

Thou Art My Sole Guide

I bow to Thee, O unfailing Guide, the dispeller
of darkness, the giver of peace on earth.
Thou art ever-gracious, ever-blissful, ever-free,
pure and perfect.
Thou art the great purifier, Thou purifiest all.
Thou art the light of knowledge, self-luminous
Consciousness, the Light of all lights.
Thou art the illuminator of each and every-
thing; everything shines in and through Thee.
Thou art in all forms, but no form can Limit
Thee.
Thou art Infinite, Thou art Eternal.
Thou art all Bliss,
Thou leadest all to supreme wisdom and
everlasting joy.

(extempore)

In this wilderness of life, I have found Thee, O Lord, the sole guide. Who but Thee could show me the way? Who but Thee could remove the darkness that veils the knowledge of Truth? Who but Thee could make me aware of the true nature of myself? It is through Thy grace alone that I am able to walk on the spiritual path.

I have found the way, though I have not reached the goal. I will not falter. Thou art taking me by the hand. If the child holds the father by the hand, the child may fall. But if the father holds the hand of the child, the child cannot fall. Thou art guiding me, Thou art protecting me. I shall follow Thee and Thee alone.

Thou art present in my guru. Thou hast assumed human form to guide the wandering souls. Who can be illumined, who can enlighten others, unless Thy grace, Thy saving power be manifest in him. Can the bound make others free? Can the blind lead the blind? Can the weak carry others' burdens? None but Thee can lead mortal man to immortality.

Thou art the one guru of all. Thou hast blessed me through the form of my teacher. May I hold to him as Thy visible form under all the varying conditions of life. In health and sickness, in sunshine and storm, in prosperity and calamity, in success and failure, in rise and fall may I see Thee in him.

Let not the charm of wealth, the charm of friendship, the charm of pleasure, the charm of fame and glory divert my heart from Thee. Thou art the only dependable One in this universe. Whom else shall I turn to? Thou art my sole guide, my companion, my friend, my refuge here and hereafter. Thou hast blessed me.

The scriptures say that the guru is Brahma, the guru is Vishnu, the guru is Shiva. Who but Thee can make man free from the bondage of karma, the deep-rooted impressions accumulated in many lives? Inevitable is the fruit of karma, but through Thy grace all its seeds can be burnt before they fructify.

Through the grace of the guru the veil of darkness has dropped from my eyes. I comprehend the Omnipresent in the manifold. Supreme Consciousness, pervading the whole universe, is being manifest to me.

I bow to the guru, the embodiment of Divine wisdom. I bow to him through whose grace the ocean of mortality is as easy to cross as the footprint of a cow. I bow to him, the leader of my soul, the giver of Liberation. There is no greater friend than the guru. There is no greater counselor than he. There is no greater benefactor than he. There is no greater gift than the gift of spiritual light.

May I never for a moment lose faith in the words of the guru. May I follow his instructions with all earnestness. May I serve him with loving devotion. May I ever be grateful to him. May my heart be filled with reverence for him!

The guru sets our feet on the right path. He removes all obstacles from the way. He gives instruction. He also gives the strength to follow the instruction. The pupil has only to follow the way, the goal is ahead of him. Just as a person who gets hold of one end of a long chain, at the other end of which are riches accumulated, can reach the treasure proceeding link by link; similarly the pupil proceeding step by step along the path on which the guru sets his feet, reaches the ultimate goal.

By the grace of the guru I have found the way. I must reach the goal through his guidance and protection.

Let us meditate on the Supreme Being as the ocean of self-effulgent Consciousness. This is the ocean of immortal Bliss. There is no fear of being drowned there. To be immersed in That is everlasting life. From the bosom of that Infinite Consciousness arises a form, the form of the guru, the embodiment of Divine Purity, of Divine Knowledge, of Divine Grace, of Divine Power.

Meditate on that form as seated on a thousand-petaled lotus, blooming at the center of your heart. He has assumed human form to reveal Himself unto you, to bless you, to guide you. Watch His compassionate eyes; watch His luminous form, the purest of the pure, all white, radiating peace, radiating love, radiating knowledge, radiating grace. That form dissolves into the Infinite ocean of Supreme Bliss. From there the guru arises; there the guru merges again.

> I bow down to the guru, the Supreme
> Brahman; I bow down to the guru, the Supreme
> Self, the one witness of all events; I bow down
> to the guru in human form, the embodiment of
> compassion, my guide, my friend, my refuge.
> (Visvasara-tantra)

Om, Shanti, Shanti, Shanti.
Peace, Peace, Peace unto all.

Thou Art Seated On The Lotus
Of My Heart

Thou alone art my Mother, Thou alone art my Father,
Thou alone art my Friend, Thou alone art my Companion,
Thou alone art my Knowledge, Thou alone art my Treasure,
Thou alone art my all-in-all, O God of gods!

(Pandava Gita)

There is no other mother than Thee, no other father than Thee, no other friend than Thee, no other companion than Thee, no other treasure than Thee, no other goal of knowledge than Thee. All earthly relationships are temporary and cannot therefore be real. Union and separation mark the life on the relative plane. Mother and father I have had life after life. Friends and companions have come and gone. Treasures I have gained and lost. They do not satisfy me. My heart craves for the eternal, the ideal, the perfect.

Thou art the eternal and perfect Mother. Thou art the eternal and perfect Father. Thou art the eternal and perfect Friend, Thou art the eternal and perfect Companion. There is no separation from Thee. Thou art all-loving, all-merciful, all-forgiving. Thou art the supreme Treasure. On attaining Thee, there remains nothing more to attain. Thou art the sole goal of knowledge. On knowing Thee there remains nothing more to know.

Thou art more than the mother, more than the father,

more than the friend, more than the companion, more than the treasure, more than the object of knowledge. Thou art my innermost Self, the Soul of my soul. Yet I do not see Thee. What a pity! Though nearest of all, Thou seem to be farther than the farthest. The seers see Thee right within the heart, but the ignorant find Thee nowhere. Pray remove from my heart all darkness and delusion, all fears, weaknesses and agonies. Make me free from all that are disruptive and destructive. Grant me strength, purity, wisdom, faith and devotion. Manifest Thyself unto me. May I see Thee within me and around me. Let us meditate on God as our innermost Self.

> The sage shakes off pain and pleasure as he realizes through meditation on the innermost self that eternal, all-pervasive, incomprehensible Being Who lies hidden in the cavern of the body inside the cavity of the heart.
>
> (Ka.U. II:12)

In the luminous space within the heart the Supreme Consciousness is manifest as the self-intelligent ego. The heart is the soul's secret chamber. We can find the omnipotent, omniscient, eternal, infinite Being right within our heart. "I am seated in the hearts of all," says Sri Krishna.[1]

Think that the atmosphere around you is animated by the Divine presence. The air that you are inhaling is wholesome, pure, serene and blissful. Think that as you inhale the air, your body is being purified through and through, all ailments and weaknesses are being chased away.

[1] B.G. XV:15.

You feel the body lighter than usual. It is refreshed and revivified, as if you have a new body, healthy, strong and pure.

Think of the body as the very temple of God. Within this temple in the shrine of the heart the Divine Lord is ever manifest as the Light of Consciousness. We do not perceive Him simply because of the mists and clouds prevailing in the mental horizon, just as on a cloudy day the sun does not appear, though shining in the sky in all its splendor.

Think that as you turn your thoughts on God you perceive His light within your heart, though you do not see Him. The divine radiance is dispersing all mists and clouds from within you. The mind appears pure and bright. With purity it attains calmness. There cannot be a pacification of the mind without its purification.

Imagine the mind as a lake with crystal pure water, absolutely calm, free from all ripples and eddies. The divine effulgence rests upon it. This lake represents the ideal state of your mind. The mind being constituted of sattvika elements (pure and subtle material substance) is intrinsically calm and transparent. It can reflect or transmit the light of Divine Consciousness.

As you watch the lake of the mind with placid surface, radiant with the light of the spirit, you find a blooming lotus at the center. It is a beautiful flower of many petals, all white, fresh and fragrant. This lotus symbolizes your heart's devotion to God. It is the most precious of all the treasures that you can have in this life. It is the seat of God within your heart. Visualize the lotus as the most beautiful thing you have ever seen. The lotus of devotion grows within the heart as you open your mind to God and His light dawns upon it and disperses darkness.

As you watch the lotus within the heart you see the Divine Lord seated on it in a form of ideal beauty, radiating love, wisdom, power, beauty and peace. Out of compassion for you the formless, featureless Divine Being has assumed form so that your mind can grasp Him. This is the form of the Formless One, an embodiment of Divine Consciousness, Divine Bliss crystallized.

Meditate on this Divine form, showering blessings upon you with upraised hands, watching you with compassionate eyes, greeting you with the sweetest words. Meditate on Him as your All-in-All, as the sole Goal and Abode, until your mind becomes completely merged in Him and you realize Him as your very self.

> One without a second, Thou art the Supreme Self indwelling in all. Thou art the Truth, self-effulgent, all blissful, eternal, immutable, limitless, stainless, matchless, deathless, decayless, without beginning and without end, free from limitations, perfect.
>
> (S.B. X:14.23)

Om, Shanti, Shanti, Shanti.
Peace, Peace, Peace unto all.

By Losing Yourself You Find Yourself

> He is the Self of Nature and the souls, the
> Supreme Ruler, the Protector of the universe,
> ever-existent, all-knowing, all-pervading, who
> governs the world eternally [throughout its crea-
> tion, continuance, and dissolution]. There is no
> other Ruler but He.
>
> He who created in the beginning the cosmic
> being and delivered to him the Vedas [the
> treasury of spiritual knowledge], who is partless,
> flawless, stainless, immutable and tranquil,
> who is the sublime bridge for reaching immor-
> tality, and resembles fire consuming fuel [as the
> destroyer of ignorance], to that effulgent Being,
> the Revealer of Self-Knowledge, I, a seeker of
> liberation, resort for refuge.
>
> (Sv.U. VI:17-19)

Man's ignorance about God is the sole cause of his bondage; so the knowledge of God alone makes him free. Being ignorant of God and the true nature of the Self, he identifies himself with the body, the senses, the mind and their aggregate. He uses the terms "I" and "mine" with regard to them and asserts himself as a distinct individual.

This egoism binds him to the world through attachment and aversion. Impelled by likes and dislikes, he performs various deeds — good and bad; meets with different situations — painful and pleasant; and harbours multiple thoughts and feelings — high and low. All these leave on his mind indelible impressions, which remain there as latent forces, become mature in the course of time and create new conditions of life here or hereafter.

As a man sows, so he reaps. Bound by the Law of Karma, he moves up and down in the phenomenal existence from one kind of life to another, repeatedly experiencing birth and death, rise and fall, hope and fear, joy and sorrow. There is no release from this chain of duality as long as he retains his egoistic self that separates him from God, his innermost, real Self.

"When the ego dies, all troubles cease," says Sri Ramakrishna. But it is very difficult to get rid of this ego. It has many forms, gross and subtle. You may subdue it in one form, yet it will reappear in another, perhaps subtler than the former. The only way to eliminate it is to surrender it completely to God, who is the one Self of all selves, the sole Master of the Universe, through whose grace alone one can be free from blinding ignorance and cross the ocean of mortality.

In order to surrender oneself to God one must be thoroughly convinced of the falsity of the egoistic self, give up all sense attachment created by it, and accept God as the supreme Goal. A person may seek God for worldly gain or even heavenly enjoyments, but this will not help him to gain freedom. A seeker of liberation must know God to be the Soul of his soul, the be-all and end-all of existence; by attaining whom there remains nothing more to attain; by knowing whom there remains nothing more to know. When the spiritual aspirant realizes God as his very Self then only he becomes absolutely free.

But the divine nature of the Self cannot be experienced by mere book knowledge or intellectual speculation. The seeker of God must adore Him and meditate on Him as the life's Ideal with faith and devotion. This is what distinguishes a spiritual aspirant from an intellectual inquirer about God. One may seek God, investigate into the nature of the Supreme Being earnestly and assiduously for academic or pragmatic interest, just as a mere philosopher or research student of religion usually does. Such a person will have only indirect knowledge of God. He cannot realize God, because he is not ready to surrender his ego and seek God as the very Goal of life. To him God-realization is not the supreme end, or the highest value. Trammeled by egoistic views and attitudes, his mind does not become clear and calm enough for the direct and unobstructed vision of Truth.

Whereas the spiritual aspirant who knows that his ego has a seeming existence, that its reality depends on the reality of God, that essentially it is one with the Supreme Being, readily surrenders himself to God and seeks Him heart and soul, worshipping Him as his very Self. His whole being turns to God. He constantly thinks of Him and meditates on Him intently. His mind becomes absorbed in God and receives the direct light of the Self, which removes all darkness from within, clarifies his vision, and reveals unto him the Truth that the Self is God. Thus by losing himself (his ego) in the Godhead, he finds himself (the Self) to be That.

"Seek, and ye shall find," says Jesus Christ. So it is declared by the Upanishads:

> This Self cannot be attained by the study of the Vedas or the power of intellect or vast learning. He who seeks the Self attains It through that seeking. To him the Self reveals Its very being.   (Ka.U. II:23; Mu.U. III:2,3)

Think that God is the sole Reality, the one substance of all changing forms, physical and psychical. It is His reality that makes everything appear as real. Without Him all is shadowy and valueless. He alone is Self-existent, Self-aware, immutable, eternal, absolutely free, pure, perfect and blissful. By realizing Him one attains self-fulfillment. "He who knows that Highest Brahman verily becomes Brahman," declares the *Mundaka Upanishad* (III:2.9), because Brahman is his very Self.

Think that He is shining in the depth of your being as your innermost Self. You do not see Him simply because you do not seek Him. Deluded by ignorance, you have mistaken the ego for your Self. At the present stage of consciousness you are virtually a psychophysical finite being, subject to birth and death, growth and decay, hunger and thirst, heat and cold, pain and pleasure and so forth. To all appearance you are bound and separate from God. But you must proceed from where you are. None but the Free One can make the bound free.

So you must approach Him the Supreme Master for liberation, and surrender yourself, that is, your ego, the cause of your finiteness and bondage. This is how you can obtain His grace. This is how the knowledge of the Real Self will dawn upon you.

Imagine that the light of the Self is appearing on the horizon of your mind, removing all darkness and delusions and transforming your ego-consciousness. As you visualize that light, think that you are neither the body nor the mind, but their knower, the experiencer of physical and mental events, a luminous being, a spark of that Light. Meditate deeply on the light of the Self proceeding from the depth of your being and permeating the mind — enveloping your finite self and absorbing it until there remains no gulf between the individual and the real Self. Then far beyond the body, the senses and the mind, you will experience one Self, limitless, free, blissful.

> Finer than the fine, greater than the great, the Self dwells in the heart of every living being. One free from desires, with the senses and the mind tranquil, sees the glory of the Self and goes beyond sorrow.
>
> (Ka.U. II:20)

Om, Shanti, Shanti, Shanti.
Peace, Peace, Peace unto all.

The Body Is Like A Garment

May my body, my organs of action, my organs
of perception, my vital principle, my mind, be
the fit instruments for the realization of Brahman,
the Supreme Truth.

My all my limbs, my eyes, my ears, my organ of
speech, each and every part of the physical system
and my thoughts and feelings be vigorous,
vitalized, so that they can help me to attain the
Supreme Being.

Brahman, the Supreme Being, self-effulgent, is
the Ultimate Reality. He sustains and manifests
the manifold.

May I never deny Brahman, may Brahman
never deny me. May there be no denial at all.

May all the virtues stated in the Upanishads
dwell within me, who am a seeker of Brahman,
who am devoted to Brahman.

(S.V.)

The Supreme Being is the very essence of the universe.
He is Pure Consciousness, Self-effulgent, Pure Bliss.
Ultimate Reality is the ideal existence — Pure Being, Pure
Consciousness, Pure Bliss. That inner bliss, self-effulgent, is
not affected by the varying physical and psychical
conditions we experience in this world. That transcends the
phenomenal existence. Unchanging, That sustains all
changes. Unobserved, That observes everything.

That self-effulgent Being is shining within us as the
conscious spirit that is our real self. Let us relax the body

and the mind, gather our thoughts and meditate on the Divine Being in the depth of our heart.

The Divine Being is omnipresent. He is the Reality in all that appear to be real. The forms appear and disappear, but the underlying Reality ever remains the same. That Reality is self-luminous, self-existent.

Our real self is the conscious spirit shining within. It is described in the Upanishads as the Life of the life, the Mind of the mind, the Eye of the eye, the Ear of the ear. That self-shining principle enlivens the body, enables the mind to think, to know. That enables the eyes to see, the ears to hear, the hands to work. That is the very center of human personality.

The body grows and decays, but the spirit within is changeless. The body feels hunger and thirst, heat and cold, but the spirit within is beyond all these changes. The mind has pain and pleasure, virtue and vice, ignorance and knowledge, but this self-shining spirit is beyond all these conditions. Dwelling in the psychophysical system and still beyond all the states of the physical body and the mind, this self-shining spirit is ever-pure, ever-free, beyond all the physical and psychical conditions.

The self-shining spirit is essentially one with the Supreme Being. As you deeply meditate on this conscious spirit, as you identify yourself with this conscious spirit, you no longer find yourself confined within the body and the mind. You feel you are transported to the realm of the self-shining Spirit, the omnipresent Being. This manifoldness disappears in the unity of the Supreme Spirit. You realize One Supreme Being, limitless, effulgent — purity itself, freedom itself, peace itself, joy itself — one existence.

That fullness of Existence is not divided by this manifoldness. The finite existences make no division in the fullness of Pure Spirit. That shines the same throughout all this diversity. In and through everything the Supreme One shines. That Supreme One is directly manifest within you as conscious spirit, as your very soul.

Turn your thoughts inward, meditate on the conscious self as the very center of your personality. Birth and death characterize the mind. Beyond the dualities of good and evil there is the self-shining spirit ever manifest, ruling over this psychophysical system, yet unaffected by all the conditions of the psychophysical system.

Meditate on the source of all light. Identify yourself completely with that. Because you forget your true self as immortal spirit, because you identify yourself with the psychophysical complex, you delude yourself with the idea that you are a mortal, that you are subject to hunger and thirst, heat and cold — that you have so many necessities in life. As long as this delusion continues you cannot be free, you must be bound. The moment you realize your self as pure spirit, you no longer find yourself confined within this psychophysical constitution. You become one with immortal spirit. You enter into everlasting life; you enter into absolute peace and freedom. You become one with the Supreme Being.

Meditate on that pure spirit as your very self, the Life of your life, the Mind of your Mind, the Eye of your eye, the Ear of your ear. Meditate on That, identify yourself with That. Think that this physical body, this psychophysical system is just like a garment which you have worn for the time being. Essentially you are pure spirit, the knower of the psychophysical system. Just as you observe physical events and the physical conditions of the body, so you observe all the mental states. You, the observer, must be distinct from all that is observed.

Meditate on this observing, perceiving Self, of the nature of pure consciousness — self-luminous. You are essentially an effulgent spirit, birthless, deathless, ageless, beyond hunger and thirst, beyond all strength and weakness. Pure Spirit is Strength itself, Purity itself, Bliss itself.

Meditate on That as a flame of light ever shining within, the Light that never flickers, the Light that never gets dim. In this way you realize your essential unity with the Supreme Being. This is the direct approach to the Supreme Reality. All other ways are indirect ways.

Right within you He is shining as your innermost self. Turn your thoughts inward, visualize the spiritual self as a flame of light shining with constant effulgence at the very center of your being. He, the Supreme Spirit, is dwelling within every heart as the individual self. Just as each and every wave belongs to the ocean, similarly each and every conscious spirit belongs to the Supreme Spirit, the Limitless One.

The whole universe is filled with the Divine Presence. You live in Him, you move in Him, you have your being in Him. You become a perfect instrument of divine power, divine love, divine knowledge, divine joy.

Others see what you have attained through devotion, through the practice of meditation, and your life becomes a blessing for humanity. This is how the great saints and seers moved the world. Their life was a blessing to one and all.

The source of all joy, of all wisdom, of all freedom is right within your heart. There is one and only one place where man meets God — it is in the depth of the heart.

> That great, unborn Self, which is identified with the intellect and which dwells in the midst of the organs, lies in the akasa [ether or space] within the heart. It is the Controller of all, the Lord of all, the Ruler of all. It does not become greater through good deeds or smaller through evil deeds. It is the Lord of all, the Ruler of all beings, the Protector of all beings . . . Knowing It alone one becomes a sage.
>
> (Br.U. IV:4.22)

Om, Shanti, Shanti, Shanti.
Peace, Peace, Peace unto all.

Blessings Of The Saints

May we hear with our ears what is good and
auspicious, may we see with our eyes what is
good and auspicious, may we live the life allotted
to us with our hearts devoted to Thee, O Lord.
(Ath.V.)

Think that everything is favorable to your spiritual life.
You are receiving the blessings of all the sages and saints of
the world. They are constantly sending their good thoughts,
their blessings, to one and all. This world is never without
spiritual vibrations, however rotten it may appear to be.
When you turn your thoughts to God, when you think of the
sages and saints of the world, when you desire to have the
Divine Light and want to develop devotion to God, then
your mind becomes open to spiritual influences that are in
the atmosphere around us. You can receive the blessings of
the great saints and seers of the world just by turning your
thoughts towards them.

When you think of worldly objects, when your mind is
filled with secular thoughts and ideas, you expose yourself
to worldly influences. Similarly when you turn your
thoughts to God, to the sages and saints of the world, to
spiritual values, your mind becomes open to spiritual
influences. Then divine blessings, divine bliss descend upon
you.

The grace of the Lord is ever ready to descend upon you,
but you do not open your mind towards the Lord's blessings

and grace. You simply turn away your mind and your thoughts from the Divinity. The sunlight is ever ready to enter into your room, but you keep the blinds closed tight, hermetically sealed as it were. How can the Divine Light enter into your heart? Turn your thoughts towards the highest as much as you can. Each time you look unto Him, His light penetrates you more or less; each time you seek divine grace, His grace descends upon you more or less. Make it a habit of turning your thoughts towards God whenever it is possible.

Your thoughts are tied down, your mind is completely chained to this sense world. Even though you try to turn your thoughts toward God you do not succeed. Yet, to the extent you try, to that extent God's light, God's grace penetrate you. Nothing can be attained in this world without effort. Whether you struggle for secular values or spiritual ideals, you have to work for any kind of achievement.

The Divine Lord is not far away from us. He dwells within man as the inmost self. Through the blessings of the saints and seers, through the grace of the Divine Lord, through your own efforts for self-purification, spiritual consciousness dawns upon you. You understand the importance of spiritual values. The secular ideals tie you down to this world of uncertainties. You can lose them at any time, any way, any where. Still you are trying to rely on the unreliable, to find security in the insecure.

If you try to get out of this situation and become convinced of the importance of spiritual life, you follow the disciplinary courses, and gradually you will develop spiritual consciousness. You realize the importance of spiritual values. Systematically you continue the practice.

As you develop spiritual consciousness you will know that you are beyond death, beyond birth, beyond growth, beyond decay, beyond all the changing conditions of the body and the mind.

You are distinct from this psychophysical organism, you are immortal pure spirit. You do not belong to this physical universe controlled by good and evil forces. You do not belong to the realm of the mind, the playground of good and evil forces. You belong to the Supreme Spirit that sustains the whole universe. As the consciousness of your spiritual self dawns upon you, you perceive your relationship with the Divinity, and are aware that He dwells everywhere in this universe.

He is the innermost reality, and you have an innermost relationship with Him. He is your Eternal Father, Eternal Mother, Eternal Friend, Eternal Companion. All worldly relationships are intended to develop within you this consciousness that your eternal relationship is with One and One only, that is God.

Birth after birth you have parents, birth after birth you have children, birth after birth you have friends. All these are intended to convince you of the fact that your Eternal Father, your Eternal Mother, your Eternal Companion, your Eternal Friend is One; and That is the Soul of all souls, That is the innermost Self of the universe. With Him you have an eternal relationship.

Hold to that Eternal Father, Mother, Friend, Companion, and everything will be meaningful. You will realize Him as your innermost self; even before leaving this body you will be in Him. His light will penetrate you, guiding you constantly. You will move in the path of light. Divine strength, divine purity, divine wisdom, divine joy will fill you through and through.

Think of the Divine Being dwelling within your heart and meditate on Him through whatever form appeals to you, whatever form represents the Divine Being to you. Through deep meditation you will realize Him.

> There is one Supreme Being who is eternal in the midst of the non-eternal, who is the one source of consciousness of all sentient beings. Though one, He creates the manifold. He fulfills the desires of one and all. Eternal abiding peace belongs to those wise persons who realize Him in the depth of the heart as the inmost self. Eternal abiding peace belongs to none else, to none else.
>
> (extempore)

Om, Shanti, Shanti, Shanti.
Peace, Peace, Peace unto all.

He Dwells In The Depth Of The Heart

> In the golden case of your inner consciousness
> is the Supreme Self, ever-shining, purest of the
> pure, all white. This is the Light of all lights, This
> is the Omnipresent Being shining within the
> heart as your innermost self. By knowing the self
> you know That, the Infinite One.
>
> (Mu.U. II:2.9)

Think that the atmosphere around you is wholesome, pure and serene. Think that you are inhaling from the atmosphere something purifying and uplifting. Think that as you inhale the air, your body is being purified through and through. All its impurities, all its weaknesses are being wiped out. All weariness and excitement have left the body. It feels lighter than usual. Your nerves are soothed. You feel refreshed and regenerated.

Think that the body has become perfectly calm and steady. It no longer offers any resistance to the quietness of the mind. Think that the mind is getting purer as it turns to God, the Light of all lights. It becomes more and more quiet at the same time, because all its restlessness is due to the impurities adhering to it.

How is the mind purified? Its impurities arise from ignorance. Darkness prevailing within the mind causes all its weaknesses. The only cure for darkness is light. When you let the light of the Supreme Spirit enter into your mind, then it becomes purified. Being purified, it becomes pacified. No pacification of the mind is possible without its purification. The more you think of God, the purer you become, the more your thoughts become concentrated on Him.

How will you meditate on Him? He is all-pervading. He is in all forms. He is also beyond forms. He inhabits the entire universe. He is also beyond the universe. He holds time and space in His bosom. He is also timeless and spaceless. How will you hold the Supreme Being within your mind, who is the All-powerful, All-knowing Creator and Preserver of the universe, Whom thoughts cannot reach, Whom speech cannot express? How will you meditate on the Supreme Being?

It is true that the Supreme Lord is present everywhere, that He is formless, featureless, beyond time, beyond space. But He is also manifest within your heart as your innermost self. Right here in the depth of the heart His light is constantly shining. In order to realize Him you will not have to go anywhere. Nowhere can you find Him but in your heart. It is in the depth of your heart that you can know Him directly, most intimately.

Vain is your search in the mountain cave, on the beautiful landscape, in the snowy peaks, in the expanse of the deep blue waters, in the flowering meadows, in the starry heaven. Nowhere can you reach Him. Everywhere you can see His manifestation, but not Him. His very manifestations hide Him from you. The Supreme Lord, who manifests and sustains the universe, has hidden Himself by His own glory, as it were. We see only His manifestation.

Turn your thoughts inward, into the inmost depth of your being. There He is shining as your very self, as the Soul of your soul. Deep within your heart there is a luminous space, the seat of your intellect, your right knowledge. Visualize the luminous space within your heart. Here is the very center of your personality. Here is the very basis of your being. Meditate on that luminous space, as the region of your self-awareness, as the abode of your spiritual self.

It is the light of the conscious spirit shining within the heart that rules over the mind and body, that controls all the senses. It is the light of the conscious spirit that enables the eyes to see, the ears to hear, the hands to work, the legs to move, the mouth to speak. In deep sleep, when the radiance of consciousness recedes from the body and the sense-organs, the senses cease to operate, and the body becomes inert. This light of consciousness emanates from your spiritual self dwelling within the heart. This light is the source of all your knowledge and love, all your goodness and greatness.

Visualize that light of consciousness within your heart and meditate on your innermost self, the changeless spirit that witnesses all the changes of the body and the mind. It shines with constant effulgence that never flickers, that never gets dim. In waking, in dream, and in deep sleep it is ever the same.

Visualize the luminous space within your heart and intensely meditate on your spiritual self, until you identify yourself with that, until you feel that you are not the physical body but the radiant spirit.

You were young some years ago. You think you have grown in size. But it is the body that grows, that decays, that has birth and death. Ageless, birthless, deathless, decayless is the luminous self. Unchanging it appears to change, being identified with the changing conditions of the body.

Unchanging it appears to change, being identified with the changing conditions of the mind. The same light expressing itself differently through different mediums undergoes no change. Forget that you are the body, that you are a psychophysical being. Realize yourself as pure spirit.

Meditate on the luminous self shining in the depth of your heart. As you identify yourself with this, you no longer find yourself confined within the mind or the body. You transcend all limitations. Behind each and every wave there is one ocean. If you look beyond the wave form that seems to separate it from the ocean, you recognize its oneness with the ocean.

The spiritual self shining within your heart is not limited by it. This is essentially one with the same Supreme Spirit that manifests the universe. It is egoism that creates a seeming difference between the individual consciousness and the universal consciousness. You are not the finite form that the wave has assumed. You are the very substance of which the wave is formed. You are of the essence of consciousness. Forget the limiting form. Realize your essential unity with the Supreme Consciousness.

The moment you withdraw from the body, the senses and the mind, and realize yourself as the pure spirit that has no circumference, you find yourself united with the Supreme Being, unbounded by space, unbounded by time. In this realm there is no past, no present, no future. It is Absolute Consciousness, which is perfection itself, bliss itself, one infinite existence beyond all limitation. It is an ocean of bliss where there is no trace of darkness, where death is unknown, where there is light and light alone.

You are in the Supreme Godhead. You are of That.

You are in That. You live in Him, you move in Him, you have your being in Him. But still you do not perceive yourself as you really are. Just as blind persons living and moving in the full blaze of the mid-day sun know nothing of the splendor of sunlight; similarly we live and move in Him, yet because of our spiritual blindness we are unaware of Him. Let the veil of darkness drop from our eyes. Let us realize our essential unity with the Supreme Self, which is Purity Itself, Life Itself, Light Itself, Bliss Itself.

O charming Lord, Yogin supreme, Thou art the perfect and primal Being. The universe both manifest and unmanifest the wise know as Thy body. Thou art the sole master of body, life, mind and senses of all beings.

Thou, verily, art Time. Thou art the all-pervading Being, the possessor of all glories, the Lord omnipotent and changeless.

(S.B. X:10.29,30)

Om, Shanti, Shanti, Shanti.
Peace, Peace, Peace unto all.

The One Source Of All

Let us meditate in the depth of the heart on the Supreme Being, who is the one source of all blessedness, who is the one goal of all knowledge; whom the highest deities seek, who is the unmoved mover of the universe. From Him the universe arises, by Him the universe is sustained, into Him the universe is reabsorbed.

He removes all fears and grants eternal light and absolute peace. The yogins realize Him in the depth of their hearts through intense meditation. It is by realizing Him that they go beyond all sufferings, all limitations and attain absolute peace and blessedness.

(extempore)

Let us relax the body and the mind, gather our thoughts, and meditate on the Divine Being in the depth of the heart. Think of the Supreme Being as the one source of all life, of all strength, of all wisdom, of all love, of all joy. He is the Adorable One. He seems to be far away from us, but in fact He is the nearest of the near. He is the innermost self of each and every human being. He is the Soul of our souls. In order to reach Him we have not to go anywhere. We can find Him in the depth of our heart through deep meditation.

Whatever power we have, whatever joy we experience, whatever wisdom we hold are all derived from Him. Apparently we gain joy from various objects. Apparently we gain strength from many sources. But He is the one source of all joy, of all strength. Every expression of joy is from Him. Every expression of power is from Him. We do not think of the source. The water that we get from the faucet does not come from the faucet, it has a source far away. Similarly all joys have one source, and that source is the Supreme Being.

The Supreme Being is the Supreme Self, He is the all-pervading Self. He is the innermost essence of everything. He is the underlying Reality that makes everything appear as real. Our power is limited, our joy is limited, our knowledge is limited because we do not turn to the one source of all power, all knowledge, all joy. Let us turn to that source.

The source is the Soul of all souls. Turn your inner eye to the inmost depth of your being. What do you find there? There is the conscious spirit, ever-shining. The Supreme Being is pure consciousness, the self-shining spirit that manifests everything. It is the light of spirit that enables the eyes to see, that enables the ears to hear, that enables the mind to think, to know, to feel. That conscious spirit within each and every individual is the source of all our strength, of all our joy, of all our wisdom.

And at the back of this individual spirit is the Supreme Self. Think of the Supreme Self, self-luminous, pure spirit, absolute consciousness. Meditate on that light. It is the light that brings purity, it is the light that brings strength, it is the light that brings joy, that brings love. Meditate on that self-effulgent spirit as your innermost being.

Through deep meditation you become united with Him. You reach the one source of all blessedness; you become transformed. From that source purity enters into your mind, into your body. From that source love enters into your heart. From that source joy enters into your being. From that source all wisdom flows.

Meditate on that light of the Supreme Spirit. Think that you have entered into that light, that you are suffused with that light, that you are completely transformed. There is the whole secret of purity, of true love, of true wisdom — to contact the source. How can you contact the source? By turning your thoughts towards Him, by meditating on the source with all faith and devotion.

Deeply meditate on Him until you realize your essential unity with Him.

May we know the Supreme Being, the Adorable One, who is self-effulgent, the Light of all lights. He is the Supreme Lord of all. He is the Supreme Master of all the masters; He is the Supreme Ruler of all the rulers; He is the Supreme Deity of all the deities.

(extempore)

Om, Shanti, Shanti, Shanti.
Peace, Peace, Peace unto all.

The Divine Child
(A Christmas Meditation)

> May the Supreme Lord of all who is wor-
> shipped by the Christians as God the Father, by
> the Jews as Jehovah, by the Zoroastrians as
> Ahura Mazda, by the Mohammedans as Allah,
> by the Taoists as Tao, by the Buddhists as Buddha,
> by the Vedantins as Brahman, by the Shaivas as
> Shiva, by the Vaishnavas as Vishnu, and by the
> Shaktas as Shakti, grant us Liberation — the
> cessation of all sufferings and the attainment of
> Supreme Bliss.
>
> (adapted from a Sanskrit prayer)

Today is Christmas Eve. On this blessed day nearly two thousand years ago was born a Savior of human souls, Jesus Christ, the son of God. A new era began with His advent.

It was a silent night. The shepherds were abiding in the field and keeping watch over their flock, when the angel of the Lord came upon them. As the glory of the Lord shone around them, they were sore afraid. But the angel comforted them, saying, "Fear not, for behold, I bring you good tidings of great joy, which shall be to all people. For unto you is born this day in the City of David a Savior, which is Christ the Lord. And this shall be a sign unto you, ye shall find the babe wrapped in swaddling clothes, lying in a manger."

And suddenly there was with the angel a multitude of the heavenly host praising God and saying, "Glory to God in the highest and on earth peace, good will toward men."[1]

[1] St. Luke 2:8-14.

Let us meditate on the Divine Child whose radiant smile is shining today on countless human hearts, on the mystery of whose birth men and women in Christendom have been meditating for centuries. Let us look back down through the ages to the sacred place of His birth at Bethlehem and visualize the glorious event. We see the Child wrapped in swaddling clothes, lying in a manger outside the crowded inn. A divine lustre enfolds Him, which physical eyes can hardly perceive.

There appear before us men and women, hurrying about, engrossed in their own affairs, without noticing the Divine Child lying in a manger under their very eyes. To demonstrate, perhaps, the supreme importance of the spiritual values and the utter insignificance of the material, the Son of God has come upon the earth so completely devoid of worldly power and possessions that He has nowhere to lay His head except in a manger.

There we see Mary and Joseph, standing before the manger looking intently upon the Child shrouded in divine glory and wondering who this Child might be. Their hearts are swayed by mixed feelings of joy, veneration, awe and parental affection. Gradually the divine glory withdraws, and the parents hug the Child to their bosoms as their own.

There we find the shepherds hastening to the place and rejoicing at the sight of the Holy Babe they were looking for since the angel of the Lord spoke to them about Him. They relate to Mary and Joseph "the good tidings of great joy," which the angel had brought them. They also deliver to the happy parents the great message with which the angel greeted the world at the coming of the Lord, "Glory to God in the highest, and on earth peace, good will toward men."

Whomever the shepherds meet they tell the wonderful things they have seen and heard.

There we meet the Wise Men from the East proceeding to the inn guided by the heavenly star. Lo! The star stands motionless in the blue vault right above the Babe, shedding its serene rays upon Him. As soon as they find the Child, the Magi kneel on the ground before the manger and worship Him with gold, frankincense and myrrh which they had carried with them all the way.

The star that rose that night has not yet set. With other luminaries, this Illustrious One is still shining in the spiritual firmament shedding divine rays upon millions of human hearts. The star, perhaps, symbolizes the advent of Jesus Christ upon the earth as the founder of a spiritual kingdom and bestower of heavenly light.

All the Saviors of the world — all Incarnations, Prophets and Messengers of God, all great spiritual leaders, saints and seers — are incessantly shining in the spiritual firmament as so many luminaries of various magnitudes, and shedding divine light upon men and women of different races and countries. On the birthday of a world-teacher the star that represents Him becomes ascendant, as it were.

Tonight, the star of Jesus Christ is in the ascendant. Let us open our hearts to Him. Let us receive His light with all humility, reverence and devotion. May His grace descend upon us. May He inspire us with divine love. May we be perfect as the Father in heaven is perfect.

The same God incarnates Himself in different climes and ages, among different peoples to establish a new order and fulfill the old. So says Sri Krishna:

Though I am unborn and immutable and the Lord of all beings, yet subjugating Nature, which belongs to Me, I appear as born through My mysterious power.
Whenever, O descendant of Bharata, there is decline of religion and rise of irreligion, I incarnate Myself.
For the protection of the good, for the destruction of the evil-doers, and for the establishment of religious order I am born in every age.

(B.G. IV:6-8)

The same saving power of God manifests itself in different forms as Rama, Krishna, Buddha, Moses, Zoroaster, Lao-tse, Christ and Mohammed. Some are worshipped as Incarnations, some as Prophets, some as Messengers of God. May we be able to recognize the Lord in all of them! May we be free from narrowness and limitations and realize Him in whom all is strung as a row of jewels on a thread.

Our salutations go to all the past prophets, whose teachings and lives we have inherited, whatever might have been their race, clime, or creed! Our salutations go to all those Godlike men and women who are working to help humanity, whatever be their birth, color or race. Our salutations to those who are coming in the future — living Gods — to work unselfishly for our descendants.[2]

Om, Shanti, Shanti, Shanti.
Peace, Peace, Peace unto all.

[2]"Christ the Messenger," *Complete Works of Swami Vivekananda,* Vol. IV, p.149. Advaita Ashrama, Mayavati, India: 1932.

To Be Spiritually Minded Is Life
(A Good Friday Meditation)

> The Self-existent One so created the living
> creatures that their senses look outward; they do
> not see the Spiritual Self within. Rare is the
> wise person, who desirous of immortality, looks
> inward, realizes the Spiritual Self and becomes
> free forever.
>
> (Ka.U. II:1.1)

The way to immortality is an inner approach. To be
ridden by the body-idea is death. To be devoted to the spirit,
to be animated and motivated by the spirit-consciousness is
life. So St. Paul says, "To be carnally minded is death; to be
spiritually minded is life and peace." (Romans 8:6) This is
what Jesus Christ has demonstrated by undergoing
crucifixion. It is one of the gloomiest days in human history,
yet it is called Good Friday because on that day Jesus Christ
showed that death cannot touch the spirit, that death affects
only the body, not the Divine Spirit shining within.

He did not try to defend Himself, He did not try to save
Himself. He gave up His life so that human beings can find
the way to immortality, can know that the soul is immortal.
So He says in the Gospel of St. John that He died for the
sake of His fold.

Let us turn our thoughts inward, let us hold to the
Divine Spirit shining within us. The Divine Spirit is the very
center of our personality. This principle of Consciousness

that animates the body, that enables the senses to function — this principle of Consciousness is Immortal Spirit. It undergoes no change; it witnesses all the changes. It is ever the Knower; it cannot be known. There is no other knower but That, no other thinker but That, no other worker but That. Because of That the body lives, because of That the organ of speech speaks, because of That the ears hear, the eyes see. Let us meditate on that immortal spirit.

Because we forget the spirit and become immersed in bodily urges we become subject to hunger and thirst, growth and decay, birth and death; but when we withdraw our thoughts, when we gather our scattered feelings and ideas and concentrate them on the spirit within, then we realize the spiritual self.

We see that we do not belong to this physical universe, we belong to the Supreme Spirit that pervades the whole universe — that self-shining Pure Consciousness that upholds this universe, that manifests this universe, that is at the back of this individual self. We find ourselves inhering in the Supreme Spirit, we realize our unity with the Supreme Spirit, and once we realize That we never become separated from Him.

For a person who realizes his unity with the Divine Being there is no death. Even though he may not be able to realize That, the very thought will sustain him throughout all the changing conditions of life. Know that in success and failure, in birth and death, in growth and decay, in prosperity and calamity, there is no death for you.

You are ever with the Divine Being — you are united with Him. Just as a wave ever exists in the ocean, similarly this divine self ever exists in the Supreme Spirit. Death and birth, growth and decay belong to the physical body, and not to the self. When we realize that, we attain strength, we attain purity, we attain wisdom, we attain love, we attain joy.

This is why Jesus Christ did not resist — whom will He resist? He knew that one soul dwells in all beings, so he said, "Resist not evil, return good for evil, love your enemies, bless those that curse you, do good to them that hate you, pray for them which despitefully use you and persecute you."[1] This is the message that Jesus Christ has given. This is the message that He has exemplified by His crucifixion. The cross is the symbol of His love and forgiveness.

Let us meditate on that event; let us meditate on the pure spirit that shines within us. Let us realize the spirit, let us go above the body. It is the body that corrupts; the spirit is changeless, ever-pure and self-effulgent. Meditate on the pure spirit. Know that you are immortal being, unchanging, pure and free, that you belong to the infinite ideal existence.

This body is just like a garment you have put on for the time being, which you slough off in the course of time. You can have another body, but as long as you are ridden by the body-idea, as long as you are carnally minded, as St. Paul says, you are in the grip of death.

But the moment you raise your thoughts, lift yourself to the realm of the spirit and become spiritually minded and devoted to the Divine Spirit, you are above death. Even though you may wear a body, even though apparently you may undergo birth, growth, decay and death, still, you are deathless, because you realize the Supreme Spirit, the Ideal

[1]St. Matt. 5:39, 44.

Existence, the Immortal, Eternal One — around you, above you, below you.

Sri Krishna says in the *Bhagavad Gita*, "The Imperishable One, the Omnipresent Being — He pervades the whole universe — nothing can destroy That." Forms undergo destruction, but the essence of Reality that pervades the universe is changeless.

The Vedic Sage declares,

> Hear me, O children of Immortal Bliss, those
> that dwell in this universe, those that dwell in
> the worlds beyond, hear me; I have realized that
> Supreme Being, the Self-effulgent One, beyond
> all darkness, resplendent like the glorious sun.
> By knowing Him alone one goes beyond death.
> There is no other way out of death.
>   (Sv.U. II:5; III:8)

Om, Shanti, Shanti, Shanti.
Peace, Peace, Peace unto all.

Think Of Yourself As An Effulgent Being

> I meditate on the Supreme Being on the lotus
> of my heart. He is self-luminous, pure conscious-
> ness. He shines within me as my innermost
> self. He, the Soul of the universe, is the soul of each
> and every one of us. He is the Light of all lights.
> He manifests and sustains the universe. He is
> the one goal of all knowledge.
> He removes all darkness, all fears, all miseries
> due to repeated births and deaths. The great
> deities seek Him, the yogins realize Him through
> deep meditation in the depths of their hearts.
> It is by realizing Him that they go beyond all
> sorrows, all limitations. They become perfect, as
> the Divine Being is perfect.
>
> (extempore)

Think that the Divine Lord is shining within your heart as your innermost self. He, the Soul of the universe, is the soul of each and every one of us. What is innermost in the universe is innermost in all of us. It is His light that is manifest within us as our innermost self. It is because of that light that we live. It is because of that light that we see. It is because of that light that we hear, we feel, we think, we know.

Each and every physical movement, each and every mental movement has been possible because of the influence of the spiritual self. When the light of the spiritual self recedes from the body, the body becomes inactive, the senses cannot function. When the light of the self recedes from the mind, the mind cannot cognize anything and we experience sleep.

Let us meditate on that light, the light of the spirit within us. That is the very center of our personality, that is our real self. This physical body is just like a garb we have put on for the time being. The garb changes, but the embodied self does not undergo any change. Meditate on that pure spiritual self as birthless, deathless, decayless, painless, untouched by hunger and thirst, heat and cold.

We forget the true nature of the self and identify ourselves with the physical body. Therefore we suffer. This physical body is just like a vehicle which we can use for the attainment of freedom. Through this physical body we can realize the true nature of the self.

The right activities, the right thinking purify the body and the mind and reveal unto us the true nature of the self. We have to conduct all the activities of the body and the mind with full awareness of the spiritual self. The more we remember the spiritual self, the more the light of the spirit shines upon the body and the mind. Then all our activities, all the movements of the body and the mind flow in right directions.

Let us deeply meditate on the spiritual self. Let all darkness that veils the nature of the self be removed. As the veil that hides the true nature of the self is removed, the body and the mind receive the direct light of spirit.

The light that is responsible for knowledge is also responsible for ignorance. The light that is responsible for correct thinking is also responsible for wrong thinking. Without consciousness we cannot think at all. The same light is responsible for wrong deeds and also for right deeds. We can think rightly, we can work rightly, only when the light of the spirit moves directly, when the veil of ignorance and darkness is removed.

By constant meditation on the true nature of the self, the veil of ignorance is removed and the light of the spirit shines with all its effulgence. Then all the operations of the body and the mind become true, become the manifestations of the Divine Spirit.

Think that the light of the spirit is shining within you. The veil of ignorance is withdrawn. You feel yourself as an effulgent being. Your body is filled with the light of the spirit, your mind is filled with the light of the spirit. You are moving in light, you are entering into the realm of light because the Supreme Reality, the self-effulgent Spirit, encompasses the whole universe.

Around you, above you, below you, within you, there is one effulgent Being, the Ocean of Blessedness. The light that shines within you also shines throughout the universe. The moment the light within you removes the darkness of the mind, the Light that is within and without penetrates you and you live in an ocean of effulgent bliss.

> I bow down to that effulgent Being who is in fire, who is in water, who is everywhere, who pervades the whole universe, who is in trees, in plants. To that effulgent Being I bow down.
> (Sv.U. II:17)

Om, Shanti, Shanti, Shanti.
Peace, Peace, Peace unto all.

PART TWO

Methods of Meditation

CHAPTER I

Introductory:
Four States of Human Experience —
Waking, Dream, Dreamless Sleep, and
Samadhi

We are all familiar with the three states of daily experience: waking, dreaming, and dreamless sleep. A normal human being experiences these three states every day, but they do not make any vital change in his way of life. He still remains in the same plane of duality, despite all the greatness he may achieve in this world. A famous scientist, a great philosopher, a politician, or a businessman does not necessarily rise above this plane of duality, this playground of good and evil forces. The panorama of growth and decay, life and death, pain and pleasure, knowledge and ignorance continues to be the same for us all until we attain the superconscious experience.

This experience induces a complete change in human life. A person becomes illumined. He becomes free from all limitations and weaknesses; he realizes his essential unity or identity with the Supreme Being. He is free from hate, all his doubts are dispelled, all his fears removed, all his weakness obliterated. Thus, a man becomes free in every sense of the word. While waking, dreaming, and dreamless sleep are common to all human beings, the superconscious state is exceedingly rare. Even after following a long and strict spiritual course of instruction, only a few individuals reach this state.

Swami Vivekananda once noted the distinction between sleep and samadhi. From the former state, he explained, a man comes out the very same as he went in, but from samadhi a man emerges a sage. His whole character is changed. These are the two vastly different effects. Now, if the effects are different, the causes must also be different. The experience attained by samadhi is greater than that gained from the unconscious or the conscious reasoning state. It must therefore be superconscious; thus, samadhi is called the superconscious state.

In the waking state a person realizes himself as a distinct individual. His self-consciousness is quite marked. He knows where he is, what he is, and so he asserts himself: "I am a man"; "I am dark" or "I am fair"; "I am tall" or "I am short"; I belong to such-and-such family"; "I belong to such-and-such nation." He is immediately aware of his present situation. This "I-ness" is the ego. A man is particularly bound by ego-consciousness in the waking state. But the ego is not the real man, for it is the real man identified with the body-mind complex. Through the ego a person identifies himself with everything he contacts.

What is the real man? The real man, having body-consciousness, is a knower of this body; but he is not the body. Just as most of us are aware of the world around us, we are also aware of the conditions of the body and the conditions of the mind. Being the knower of the body and the mind, we are beyond them both. We are basically the knower. The knower has consciousness inherent in him.

Consciousness is his very essence. A ray of light does not know itself, nor does it know anything else; but the spiritual light shining within us is self-aware and at the same time aware of everything else. There is the fundamental difference between spiritual light and physical light. *That* light we carry always within us, *That* is the very essence of our being.

The mind is not self-luminous because mind is objectified. Anything that is objectified has no light as its essence. This has been pointed out by the great philosopher and psychologist, Patanjali.[1] There are many Western philosophers who think consciousness belongs to the mind. But mental states are not conscious in themselves. Mind has a knower. The Self is that knower; it is the real man.

The Self, whose nature is pure consciousness, ever shines and is changeless. The knower of change undergoes no change. Changes always imply an unchanging knower. The Self is that knower: changeless, pure, free, and by nature immortal; beyond growth and decay, belonging to the Supreme Reality, and perfect. That perfection we carry always within us.

Through the modification of the mind, that essence is individualized, is characterized by "I-ness," so that whenever we recognize ourselves, we must pass through this "I." We cannot comprehend ourselves without this "I-ness," even though our "I" is not a real person. The real person is behind the "I." That ever-shining essence, through modification of the mind, is manifested as the ego. Thus the real man becomes identified with this physical body.[2]

[1] Y.A. IV:19. Patanjali lived in India during the second century, B.C.
[2] See "From Mortality to Immortality," Appendix I.

In the waking state we are conscious of two orders of facts: on the one hand we see external phenomena; on the other a procession of internal phenomena. But we cannot see the entire mind, we see only the "upper" part of it. Sometimes we feel happy, sometimes we have fears; sometimes we have hope, sometimes we have unhappiness. But within us we still carry many tendencies, desires, memories, and impressions. Only a part of the mind is revealed to the ego-consciousness. That part of the mind is generally called the "conscious mind."

In the waking state we are ridden by the body-consciousness. In the dream state the individual self moves from this physical level down to the subconscious level. Below the level of normal consciousness, in that subconscious region, reside our tendencies, yearnings and the past impressions of our experiences in life. In the waking state a person has a definite ego-consciousness. But when the individual self moves from the physical level into the subconscious level where all impressions are stored, the sense of the waking ego is lost. The self is submerged in the stored impressions, as it were.

Reasoning power and volition do not function in the subconscious state; imagination is rife and emotion is uncontrolled. Imagination creates any number of images from subtle impressions. In the dream state we are deprived of the two great powers which characterize us as human beings: reasoning power and will power. We are, indeed, at the mercy of emotion and imagination.

Then, in deep sleep, we go even farther down. Far below the dream level of the mind there is another level — the causal state. In the dream state there are diversities in the mind: love, feeling, and memory. But in the causal state all become homogeneous.

For example, take a seed, which is the causal state of the tree. In the tree we notice variations; but in the seed, which contains the tree in latent form, no variation is noticeable.

In the same way there is a causal state of the mind in each individual where all operations of the mind are completely hushed. Even the ego-consciousness becomes lost. We do not know what we are. A king is no king, a mother is no mother in that state. Complete ignorance reigns, but the individual self remains the tacit witness of that ignorance.

In deep sleep we have no will, no self-awareness at all. But when we emerge into the waking state we have all the necessary opportunities for progress. No achievement, no progress is possible except in the waking state. No progress takes place on the subconscious level because in that state there is no self-awareness.

Similar to these dream and dreamless states are the states of intoxication, of coma, or of states induced by drugs or hypnosis. They are alike the dream and dreamless states, for they lack the power of reasoning and will.

The waking state is, therefore, important for man. Whatever achievement he can effect must be in the waking state, because it is then that he has self-awareness, and this awareness creates self-determination. It is self-determination which serves as the foundation of our reasoning power and volitional power.

What distinguishes the human level from the sub-human level? The power of reasoning and the power of will. On the subconscious level, we are guided by instinct; but on the conscious level volitional action prevails. And there can be no volition without the power of judgment or reason. All progress on the human level results from this volition associated with the power of judgment. We see things, and at the same time we judge things. The eyes perceive, and the mind judges whether it is good for us or not. Pleasure, or that which is pleasant, is not necessarily good. The cultivation of intellectual life, moral life, ethical life, spiritual life — all of which distinguish a human individual — is possible only in the waking state.

Now just as the subconscious level is below the ego-consciousness, similarly, the superconscious level is *beyond* the ego-consciousness. If we want to reach the super-conscious state we have to do so by exercising our reasoning power and will power. We have to completely rid ourselves of the ego-idea, which limits us.

But by taking drugs, or submitting to other such chemical alterations of the mind, we lose that precious element of consciousness which makes us self-aware and self-determined, and enables us to cultivate our intellectual, moral, and spiritual lives. The moment we lose this self-awareness, we become "nobodies."

Instead, we must go beyond ego-consciousness. Those great spiritual leaders who have achieved the super-conscious state emphasize that the mind has a yearning for Truth. Unless the mind moves away from the temporal to the eternal, it cannot reach this Truth. "As long as there is any fiber sticking out of the thread," Sri Ramakrishna said, "it cannot pass through the eye of the needle." Persons who would overcome their yearning for transitory pleasures and, instead, cultivate a yearning for the eternal, must practice certain disciplines to achieve this superconscious state.

If we can overcome desire for that which is transitory, we can start on our way to the highest. But how do we go about it? First, we do not deviate from our moral principles. We try to be sincere, truthful, charitable, and at the same time continue to carry out our duties. In this way we get the most out of life. It is moral principle which supports our physical health. It is moral principle which is the basis of reasoning power, as well as spiritual power. The moment we deviate from moral principles we jeopardize our entire lives. So we must be firm in these principles and continue to live in our present situation. We will then get the best from life, and, at the same time, realize its inherent shortcomings. And we shall think: "Deep in my heart, I am longing for eternal life, deep in my heart I am longing for a joy inexpressible."

Can there be no evil in this world? Can we have only good and good alone? No. Evil and good are inseparable. We cannot have the one without the other. For so long as we cling to the ego, we will experience both good and evil, life and death, growth and decay, joy and sorrow. If we wish to go beyond duality — the drama of love and hatred, of smiles and tears — we must rid ourselves of the domination of ego-consciousness. The greatest spiritual leaders urge us to satisfy our inherent longing for the eternal, for peace and freedom. They teach no drastic measures. They tell us to continue to perform our duties and be fully aware of the situation in which we exist; then we may follow a spiritual course.

There are many different spiritual paths. We must develop devotion to God by doing our duties as forms of worship. We must practice both mental and physical disciplines. When a natural devotion blossoms in the heart, a person can only then effectively meditate on God. One can intellectually think that God is the supreme Ideal and hold on to Him, but unless one can develop natural and spontaneous longing for Him, meditation cannot be practiced with success.

Through deep meditation, when the mind is tranquil and serene, the perception of Reality comes. God is not merely a personal Being; He is manifest in the whole universe, He is everywhere; He is the Existence, the Absolute, the One. That Absolute is not a material existence, but the Light of all lights, ever-shining. Whatever we see in this world, we should remember that Basic Light, underlying all things at all times — that Pure Consciousness hidden beneath this manifold universe.

So declares the *Upanishad:*

> There the sun shines not, nor does the moon, nor do the stars. Nor does lightning flash there. How can this (mundane) fire? That shining everything shines because of It. Through Its effulgence all this becomes manifest.
> (Ka.U. II:2.15)

A spiritual aspirant must meditate knowing that whatever he experiences must pass through the mind. The mind is the one indispensable instrument for every kind of cognition. From the lowest to the highest, from the grossest object to the Ultimate Reality, it is through the mind that we know it. When we perceive or experience an object, there invariably occurs a modification in the mind in the form of that object. The mind conforms to the object. That is how knowledge is possible.

Suppose reference is made to some object located in India. A man hears me tell about it, and through words he receives an idea about the object. His mind conforms to the object that I am describing. The more his mind corresponds to the object the greater becomes his knowledge. In this way he gains indirect knowledge through another's testimony.

Now let us suppose he travels to India and sees the object for himself. He then gains direct experience, for his mind comes in contact with the object. In indirect knowledge the mind conforms to the object, but does not coincide with it. But in direct perception, mind conforms to the object and also coincides with the object.

In the perception of God, the same law also prevails. The more the mind is concentrated on an object, the greater its knowledge; and the more the mind conforms and coincides with that object, still greater is its knowledge. Without concentration of the mind we cannot know anything well. To have the knowledge of God we must concentrate the mind; therefore, meditation is the final stage of spiritual aspiration. All other spiritual disciplines are intended to prepare the mind for this practice of meditation. In the *Upanishad* we read:

> The Supreme Being is not perceived by the eye nor expressed by the organ of speech, nor apprehended through any other organ, nor is this attainable through austerity or by the performance of deeds. When one becomes purified in mind through the clearness of understanding then one can realize that indivisible Self through meditation.
>
> (Mu.U. III:1.8)

How can That be reached? When this mind becomes purified. And purification of understanding is possible only in the waking, conscious state. When the mind has become purified, then that mind, by practicing meditation, attains to the superconscious state and realizes that Ultimate Reality which is beyond all diversity and embraces all variations.

To prepare for this practice, one has to surrender the self. One has to think that this individual self belongs to Him. Through worship, or whatever way possible, one should try to realize a deeper relationship with Divinity. Then one will be able to practice concentration of mind.

But it is very difficult to fix the mind on something abstract. To practice concentration we use any form that represents divinity to us. Think that this form is the very embodiment of divine consciousness, love, joy, and freedom. By concentrating on this form of divinity, a person reaches the formless divinity. And when he reaches this formless aspect, the veil of ignorance is removed and the mind becomes suffused with divine light. In such a state the perception of Reality comes.

There are two distinct stages of the superconscious state: one is called *savikalpa* samadhi, the other *nirvikalpa* samadhi. In savikalpa samadhi a person realizes his deepest unity with the Supreme Being. In nirvikalpa samadhi this difference between the individual self and the supreme Self completely disappears. The seeker recognizes his identity with the Supreme Being.

We have heard it said that there is some similarity between deep sleep and samadhi. True, there is a similarity; and also a great difference. In deep sleep all the operations of the mind become completely hushed. All its fluctuations cease. In samadhi, also, all the modifications of the mind — willing, reasoning, feeling, imagination — become silent. We realize the ego as belonging to Him completely.

In savikalpa samadhi we are aware of the individual self, but it completely belongs to Him, just as a wave belongs to the ocean. But in nirvikalpa samadhi we enter into the Light of all lights. The veil of ignorance which has been hiding Reality from us is removed. The mind is flooded with light. In deep sleep there is no light. The individual self is a mere witness of ignorance. The mind is covered by a veil of darkness. All operations of the mind are hidden. We experience nothing. Ignorance is the nature of deep sleep, but in samadhi we experience one undivided consciousness, unlimited by time or space. It is Pure Consciousness.

Suppose one dreams that one has become an angel and can fly. He sees heaven, and the saints who have gone there. He sees all these things in his dream. To him it may seem an expansion of consciousness, but will that consciousness enable him to achieve anything? No. As soon as he awakens he finds himself again grumbling about the cruelty of the world!

Expansion of consciousness can only be achieved by overcoming the limitation of "I." The true Self is always shining within us. The more we meditate on that Self the more we realize that we are not the physical body, nor the mind. We are pure spirit. The more we realize this fact, the more will we feel we do not belong to this physical world, but to the limitless, supreme Reality.

We have to develop spiritual awareness, for such awareness links us with the supreme Spirit. And we can only arrive at it through moral and spiritual discipline. All the great saints and mystics of the world paid this price for their experiences. When one has realized the supreme Truth he will lead a life free from the common weaknesses of humanity, free from selfishness. He will be forever established in that Truth and Light. It is said in the *Mundaka Upanishad:*

> When He who is immanent and transcendent is perceived, directly experienced, then all doubts are dispelled. All knots of the heart that tie an individual to this sensible universe are completely cut asunder, and all the deposit of [past] karma is wiped out.
>
> (Mu. U. II:2.8)

CHAPTER II

Work and Meditation

Meditation in a general sense means deep contemplation. It requires continuous application or concentration of the mind on something in particular, objective or subjective. It can be well cultivated throughout our life — through all our deeds. There is nothing we can do, or see, or hear, or know, or understand properly, without the application of the mind. Someone may speak to you, still you will not hear him or understand him, unless your mind is fixed on his words.

Even the ordinary deeds of life, such as cooking or sweeping, cannot be well done unless the mind is fixed on the work; not to speak of higher duties of life, such as teaching a pupil, writing an essay, or painting a portrait. The more the mind is fixed on the work, the better is the result. A scientist in the laboratory must concentrate his mind on his research work. A philosopher must concentrate his mind on the problem he wants to solve. A statesman must concentrate his mind on the political issue at hand.

The power of concentration develops through steady practice. Judicious practice is the secret of progress in all walks of life. Whatever progress you make by right practice will be your permanent asset. It is through regular practice with concentration of mind that a wrestler becomes a successful wrestler, a speaker becomes a successful speaker, a writer becomes a successful writer, an artist becomes an expert artist. So concentration of mind is needed in each and every field of action.

The practice of concentration disciplines the mind. A fowler cannot shoot a bird successfully without practice, an archer or marksman cannot shoot the target without regular practice. Whenever we want to concentrate the mind on something in particular, we have to detach the mind at the same time, more or less, from all other concerns. A fisherman cannot catch fish with his rod and reel unless he watches the float very attentively.

There is a story that a man was catching fish with his rod when a passerby came to him and asked the whereabouts of a man in the neighborhood. He spoke two or three times, still the fisherman could not answer him because his mind was concentrated on the float. The passerby rebuked him for not answering for so long. After the fish was caught the fisherman begged to be excused for not hearing the question of the passerby.

In practicing concentration of the mind on something in particular both the power of attachment and detachment of the mind are necessary. You cannot fix your mind on something in particular, unless your mind is detached for the time being from all other concerns. This power of detachment requires self-mastery. The power of attachment and detachment go together. Without self-control this power cannot be acquired — it necessitates the practice of virtue. Anyone who succumbs to vices such as anger, jealousy, hatred, pride, loses control over the mind. Any kind of ill feeling impairs the mind.

It is to be noted that virtue implies fellow-feeling towards our fellow-beings; vice implies ill-feeling towards our fellow-beings. But if we develop virtues within us instead — such as kindness, truthfulness, charity, sincerity, then we can maintain self-mastery. The reason is, virtues we can practice with self-possession, while vices subjugate us. Consequently the practice of concentration in the common deeds of life requires the development of virtue.

As we have already mentioned, the power of concentration develops with steady practice. Regular systematic practice is the secret of progress in every field of life. The most difficult and the hardest task a man faces in life is the control of the mind. The secret of attaining that is continuous, persistent practice.

The problem of controlling the mind has faced human beings at all times. Centuries ago Arjuna faced the same problem. Arjuna said to Sri Krishna, "Verily the mind, O Krishna, is restless, turbulent, obstinate, and stubborn. I regard it quite as hard to gain control over the mind as over the wind."

Sri Krishna admitted the habitual restlessness of the mind and answered: "O mighty armed, there is no doubt that the mind is restless, and difficult to control; but through practice and dispassion, O Arjuna, it can be governed."[1]

Although Sri Krishna spoke with reference to spiritual life, the same principles of the control of the mind applies to the secular life as well. The key to the control of the mind in practical life is the persistent effort to dwell on the matter at

[1] B.G. VI:34,35.

hand, leaving aside, for the time being, all else.

Patanjali in his *Yoga Aphorisms* mentions the same principles regarding the control of the mind as stated by Sri Krishna.

"Through practice and dispassion the fluctuations of the mind are controlled."

"Continuous struggle to subdue them is practice."

"This power of concentration becomes firm through long-continued, steady practice with fervor."[2]

The continuous application of the mind on a particular theme is like the unbroken flow of oil poured from one vessel to another. Another illustration is when the mind is concentrated fully, it becomes one-pointed like the flame of an oil lamp kept in a windless place.

Arjuna was the best arrowman of the age. In ancient times the chief weapons of warfare were the bow and arrow. The best warrior was he who was the most expert archer.

It is said that a teacher of archery thus tested his students after they had been trained for some time. The teacher called one of the students and asked him, "Can you shoot that distant bird?" (The bird was seated on one of the top branches of a distant tree.)

"Yes," replied the pupil.

"What do you see when you aim at the bird?"

"I see the tree, I see the branches and I also see the bird seated on a branch."

"No," replied the teacher. "You cannot shoot the bird. Go away."

Then he asked the second student, "What do you see

[2]Y.A. I:12-14.

while aiming at the bird?"

"I see the bird," the student answered, "and the branch on which it is seated."

"Go away," said the teacher.

Then the teacher called the third student. "Can you shoot the bird?"

"Yes."

"Aim at the bird. Fix your arrow. What do you see?"

"I see only the bird. I do not see anything else."

"Shoot," said the teacher. And the student was successful in hitting the bird, which fell to the ground, dead.

Such is the one-pointed application of the mind. It leads to success.

To sum up, we can say that without practicing concentration on the gross, one cannot fix the mind on the fine. From the fine one can direct the mind to finer and finer objects. Similarly, after practicing concentration on the concrete one can concentrate the mind on the abstract.

As noted by Patanjali, after practicing concentration on the sense-objects one can meditate on the sense-organs, then on the mind and then on the self, the knower within.

The following remarks of Swami Vivekananda on the gradation of the practice of concentration are pertinent:

"We have but one method of acquiring knowledge. From the lowest man to the highest Yogin, all have to use the same method; and that method is what is called concentration. The chemist who works in his laboratory concentrates all the powers of his mind, brings them into one focus, and throws them in the elements; and the elements stand analyzed and thus his knowledge comes. The astronomer has also concentrated the powers of his mind, and brought them into one focus; and he throws them onto objects, through his telescope; and stars and systems roll forward, and give up their secrets to him.

"So it is in every case; with the professor in his chair, the student with his book, with every man who is working to know. You are hearing me, and if my words interest you, your mind will become concentrated on them; and then suppose a clock strikes you will not hear it on account of this concentration; and the more you are able to concentrate your mind, the better you will understand me and the more I concentrate my love and powers, the better I shall be able to give expression to what I want to convey to you. The more this power of concentration, the more knowledge is acquired, because this is the one and the only method of acquiring knowledge.

"Even the lowest shoe black, if he gives more concentration will black shoes better; the cook with concentration will cook a meal all the better. In making money, or in worshipping God, or in doing anything, the stronger the power of concentration the better will that thing be done. This is the one call, the one knock, which opens the gates of nature, and lets out floods of light. This, the power of concentration, is the only key to the treasurehouse of knowledge."[3]

[3]"The Ideal of a Universal Religion," *Complete Works of Swami Vivekananda,* Vol. II, p.388. Advaita Ashrama, Mayavati, India: 1932.

CHAPTER III

Search for God

Just as there are in this world seekers of transitory possessions and pleasures, such as wealth, beauty, intellectual knowledge, power; similarly there are seekers of God, the Supreme Being. The seekers of God are, of course, rare. Nevertheless, there have been seekers of the Supreme Being in this world in all ages, in all parts of the world.

It is said that Brahma, the Cosmic Person, created in the beginning four sons. Very early in life they left the world and plunged into meditation on the Divine Being. They were the followers of the path of renunciation (nivritti marga). They did not serve the purpose of creation, which also requires followers of the path of worldly pursuits (pravritti marga).

In the opening verses of the *Svetasvatara Upanishad* it is said:

> The seekers of Brahman inquired — What is the cause of the universe? Is it Brahman? Whence are we born? How do we live? Where is our ultimate Goal? At whose command, O the knowers of Brahman, are we bound by the law of happiness and suffering?

> Time, inherent nature of things, destiny, chance, the elements, primal energy, the ego — none of these, nor a combination of these, can be considered to be the cause of

the universe; because they depend on the existence of the knowing self. The self, too, cannot be the cause, for being subject to the law of happiness and suffering, it is not free.

Being absorbed in deep meditation they perceived within themselves the self-luminous Supreme Being with Its power hidden by the manifestations of Its own gunas.[1] It is He who presides over all the causes beginning with time and ending with the individual self.

(Sv.U. I:1-3)

But the seekers of God vary in their nature. All do not seek God in the same spirit. There is one class of seekers who have been in quest of God for intellectual understanding. This universe has been a riddle to the human mind from the very beginning. Howsoever engrossed a person may be in worldly affairs, some time or other he is likely to face the fundamental questions — How does this universe exist? Where does it come from? What is the goal? What is the meaning of this life? Such queries have been the mainspring of philosophical investigations.

The philosophers have tried to find God for intellectual satisfaction. Their chief instrument in this respect has been reason based on the process of inference; and it is the consensus of many philosophers that the Ultimate Reality

[1]The three gunas — *sattva, rajas,* and *tamas* — are the primal constituents of prakriti (or maya). They balance one another in its potential state. This is a state of equilibrium of the gunas. Prakriti (or maya) becomes operative with the disturbance of this equilibrium, which releases the latent force that is behind all of its manifestations. The gunas form a triad. It is the predominance of one or another in varying degrees that causes all transformations. *Sattva* is the principle of poise conducive to purity, knowledge, and joy. *Rajas* is the principle of motivity leading to activity, desire, restlessness or disquietude. *Tamas* is the principle of inertia resulting in inaction, dullness, and delusion.

cannot be comprehended through reason. Cosmological argument, or technological argument, or ontological argument does not reveal Reality to the inquirer. One cannot have the immediate experience of the Supreme Being by dialectic process or through speculation.

Then there have been other seekers who have sought God not just for the satisfaction of their intellect, but out of dire necessity. This world could not give them the satisfaction they hankered after. Howsoever real and attractive the world may appear to be, it does not appeal to many as an ideal existence. It is far short of the ideal that the human mind aspires after. Whatever man may do to make this world come closer to the ideal — despite all the dreams of inevitable progress and ever-increasing perfection, despite marvelous inventions and dexterous statesmanship — this world ever remains a welter of dualities, such as good and evil, peace and war, want and plenty, knowledge and ignorance, rise and fall.

So the question arises: how can man reach that ideal of perfection, that ideal existence which he so often dreams of. If this relative existence be the sole reality, then there is no possibility of the fulfillment of man's highest aspiration. It is not just the sentiment of wonder, or mystery, that awakens within man the urge for investigation into the cause of the universe; it is a matter of practical necessity.

This world does not insure man of the security that he is longing for. There is no assurance even of the fulfillment of his legitimate desires and ideals. So the question arises within him, "Am I destined to be ever satisfied with this world, this kind of life?" Again, he asks — "Is there true security beyond this world, or is man born to seek security in the insecure? Is death the final end, or is there life beyond death?" This is the dilemma that has turned the minds of many to the search for the Supreme Being, apart from the question of curiosity, or mystery, or intellectual satisfaction, which may have led many philosophers and theologians into investigation about the nature of the Ultimate Reality.

The Upanishadic sages declare: No, death is not your final end. Do not give way to despair. You are not destined to be subject to this play of dualities forever. There is the Supreme Being, the very perfection of existence, which you can reach in this very mortal life and where you can find life beyond death and complete fulfillment of your ideal. Therein is the culmination of your knowledge, therein is the consummation of your love, therein is complete rest and therein dwells unruffled peace. There shines the Light that never fails, and there abides joy unbounded. How can man reach that? Through this very life, by regulating his mortal life he can reach the immortal. This is the message of the world's great sages.

Not a few have followed the path of God, have been in quest of the Ultimate Reality in this spirit. As long as death prevails in this world, as long as there is no 'good' unmixed with 'evil,' there will be the search for the Supreme Being beyond dualities in human life. It cannot be prevented. This search is inherent in the human mind because man's inmost self is attuned to that.

Through good and better man is constantly seeking the best, through great and greater he is constantly seeking the greatest. Through high and higher he is constantly seeking the highest. After persistent efforts to reach the best through better and better; to reach the greatest through greater and greater; to reach the highest through higher and higher; man becomes disillusioned. He at last comes to understand that there can be numerous good and better, there can be numerous great and greater, numerous high and higher, but the Best, the Greatest, the Highest is only One. That One is the Supreme Being.

> He, Who, though One and Undiversified, creates in the beginning diversities by His manifold power and Who, at the end, withdraws them unto Himself, without any motive of His own, may that Self-Effulgent Supreme Being endow us with salutary understanding.
>
> (Sv.U. IV:1)

In the same *Svetasvatara Upanishad* there is an inspiring message for all human beings. One of the sages declares from his own experience:

> I have realized the Supreme Being, resplendent like the sun, beyond all darkness. It is by realizing Him that the mortal man becomes immortal. There is no other way out.
>
> There is nothing further or closer than He. There is nothing smaller or greater than He. Shining in His own glory He stands firm like a tree — One without a second. By that Being the whole universe is filled.
>
> The Supreme Being ever dwells in the heart of man as the inmost self, no bigger than the thumb.[2] He is recognized as the knower of the wise who discriminates the self from the not-self; the Knower from the known. Those who know Him become immortal.
>
> (Sv.U. III:8,9,13)

For the sake of God, many earnest seekers give up

[2]See "The Location of the Soul in the Body," Appendix II.

everything in this world — their dearest and nearest ones, their hearth and home, children and property — and go into seclusion, living in a forest, or on the solitary banks of rivers or in the caves of mountains. They shed tears, pray to God constantly, and contemplate on Him. After seeking God in the solitude and the sublimity of nature, as the mind is purified by the practice of austerities and constant contemplation on Him, they discover that He is right within the heart. There is just one place where man meets God — right within the heart He dwells as the innermost self. He who seems to be the farthest is the nearest of all.

An illustration has been given that just as a musk deer tries to locate the source of the fragrance of the musk that grows at its navel, so a seeker of God without the guidance of a competent teacher roams about here and there, everywhere, in order to find God dwelling within him as the inmost self.

The story is this — there is a special kind of deer called musk deer. When the musk deer becomes mature, it develops musk at its navel. The musk emits a fragrance which the deer inhales. Without knowing its source the deer is fascinated by this fragrance emitted by the musk growing at its own navel. Naturally it tries to find the source of the fragrance. In search of the same it goes here and there, roams over high cliffs and valleys; then it gets tired, lies down and all of a sudden it discovers that the source of the fragrance is at its own navel.

Similarly, the ideal of perfection, the ideal of beauty, the ideal of power, the ideal of freedom, that man constantly seeks is derived from his inmost self, because his very self is of the divine nature, ever-pure, self-luminous, immortal, free, and belongs to the Supreme Being, just as the wave belongs to the ocean.

Contrarily, there have been other seekers who have searched for God, not for the sake of God, but for the sake of something else. They have also worshipped God, prayed to God, and meditated on God. What for? For the sake of wealth, for the sake of power, for the sake of relief from dire distress in which no human help can avail. These seekers of God, also, gradually develop true devotion to God. They gradually understand that they have not to seek anything through God because God is the highest Ideal in Himself. In Him is complete self-fulfillment. He is the one source of all beauty, of all knowledge, of all power, of all joy. He is at the same time all gracious. So why should they seek something else through God?

If you go to a diamond mine will you busy yourself in gathering pebbles there? If you reach a fountain of crystal pure water, will you go on digging a well by the side of that perennial spring in order to alleviate your thirst? Similarly, no sensible person will approach the Supreme Being, the Ideal Reality, the One Source of all existence, all consciousness, all bliss, for transitory pleasures and possessions.

It is as the Vedas declare: "All beings live on a particle of that Bliss." A particle of His joy fills human hearts with joy, a particle of His love fills human hearts with love, just as a particle of His beauty endows the face of nature with beauty. If you reach that source, could you ask for perishable things, knowing that the all-gracious divine power can give you anything? It is like children asking their father for toys and dolls, knowing that the loving father can give them anything. However, these seekers of transitory pleasures develop good sense in due course. Real yearning for God comes sooner or later. Instead of seeking anything through God, they seek God Himself.

The seekers of God have followed two distinct courses, broadly speaking. The one is the path of devotion, Bhakti-yoga; the other is the path of knowledge, Jnana-yoga. In the one feeling or emotion is prevalent. In the other reasoning is predominant. Feeling and reasoning are the two main functions of the human mind. These control our actions and thoughts. Naturally our religious life has also been dominated by these two functions. Actually these are the two main approaches to the Supreme Being.

Generally speaking, both emotion and intellect prevail in the life of an individual. In some human minds emotion is predominant. In others intellect is predominant. Similarly, in the religious life also there has been the scope of reason in the path of devotion, the path of love for God. And there has been the scope of devotion, or feeling, in the path of knowledge although mainly characterized by reason. The followers of Jnana-yoga stress devotion to the spiritual teacher as indispensable. For instance, we quote the first three stanzas of Shankaracharya's hymn to the benign guru from among his devotional hymns.

Hymn to Sri Dakshinamurti[3]

I

I bow down to Sri Dakshinamurti in the form of my guru:
I bow down to Him by whose grace the whole universe appears to

---

[3]An epithet of the guru, or spiritual preceptor, in his benign aspect as the embodiment of grace and compassion.

exist within myself like the reflection of a city in a mirror,
Although through Maya like a dream imagery it appears outside;
Through whose grace again upon waking — on the Realization of
　　Truth,
It is perceived as the everlasting and nondual Self.

II

I bow down to Sri Dakshinamurti in the form of my guru:
I bow down to Him who, by the sheer power of His will,
Projects outside, like a magician or a mighty yogi,
　　this vast universe,
Which, in the beginning, rests homogeneous without name or
　　form, like the sprout in a seed,
And after creation, by virtue of time and space imagined through
　　Maya,
Appears to be the manifold, possessed of endless shapes and hues.

III

I bow down to Sri Dakshinamurti in the form of my guru:
To whom outward manifestations, though based on the Real,
　　appear as illusory, ever-changing objects;
Who grants to those who take refuge in Him through the Vedic
　　pronouncement "Tattvamasi" ("That thou art"),
The boon of immediate knowledge of Brahman,
On attaining which the seeker returns no more to the realm of
　　birth and death.

　　Those who have proceeded toward the Supreme Goal
by the path of knowledge have conceived the Ultimate
Reality as an Impersonal Absolute Being (Nirguna
Brahman) beyond all diversities. Those who have followed

the path of devotion have conceived the Supreme Being in relation to the universe, as possessed of attributes (Saguna Brahman), the Personal God. With the Personal God living beings and inanimate universe co-exist. The followers of Jnana-yoga have reached the goal through the consciousness of the identity of the individual self with the Supreme Being. This has been their final experience. The individual soul does not exist in the Ultimate Reality as a distinct entity.

In the path of devotion, in the beginning the seeker conceives God as existing far away from him. As he progresses in spiritual life he becomes aware of an intimate relationship with the Supreme Being. He comes to recognize the fact that just as God is Spiritual Reality, similarly a human individual is essentially a spiritual being. He is not just a physical being or a psychophysical being; essentially he is a spiritual entity, his real self is birthless, decayless, deathless, undying, undecaying — ever-pure, free and self-luminous.

In this way a devotee establishes a relationship, an inner relationship with the Divinity. He feels his deep kinship with God and conceives God as the Supreme Ruler, as the Eternal Father, as the Eternal Mother, as the Eternal Friend, or even as the Eternal Beloved.

As a seeker of God goes through spiritual disciplines and progresses toward the Goal he finds that God is not far from him. He is the Supreme Self immanent in the whole universe. He is not apart from anything, nothing exists independently of God. Everything is in Him. So the seeker gradually finds that at the back of each and every individual self is the Supreme Self. He is the Soul of all souls. The seeker realizes Him as the very essence of his being. He realizes the unity of the individual self with the Supreme Self.

Various preparatory courses have to be followed by the seekers of the Impersonal Being as well as by the seekers of the Personal God. Physical courses, verbal processes, mental processes make up the spiritual disciplines. Both these types of followers have followed the method of meditation. It is through deep meditation that they have realized God, directly contacted God. So the final approach to God in both these ways has been meditation. It is through meditation on the identity of the individual self with the Supreme Being that the seeker of the All-transcendent Being has reached the Goal. And it is through meditation on the unity of the individual self with the Supreme Being that the seeker of the Personal God has realized the Goal.

If you do not know your Goal, whatever progress you make is no progress, truly speaking. But if you know your Goal and if you make a single step towards it, that is also an achievement. This world in itself does not change as a whole. It remains as a playground of bright and dark forces. You may divert 'plenty' from one region to another, divert 'want' from one region to another — progress or decline may move from one place to another; but the world as a whole remains a playground of dualities. You can get moral and spiritual exercise through the right kind of life you live. Countless individuals are going beyond this plane of duality and reaching the Supreme Being.

The world is a gymnasium for our moral and spiritual exercise. It does not change very much. If you throw a ball along a bowling alley the ball comes back to you; again if you throw, again it comes back. There is no change in the bowling alley, but you are getting exercise.

Similarly, this field of action apparently is meaningless. On the whole you cannot alter it. Civilizations after civilizations have grown in this universe and again collapsed. Progress is in one section or another, and then degradation in one section or another. But human beings gain morally and spiritually if they live their lives judiciously. A gymnasium cannot be a permanent residence. It cannot be an ideal home or a permanent dwelling. So this life, though an enigma to all appearance, nevertheless serves as a stairway to reach the highest.

CHAPTER IV

Worshipping God Through Symbols as Preparatory to Meditation

Symbols have been used in all religions of the world for the purpose of apprehending spiritual truths. The fundamental Reality beyond the sensible universe has been conceived by human beings according to their tendencies and capacities, called by different names, represented by different forms, and approached by different modes of worship.

There are more symbols than one in every religion. They are not conventional, inasmuch as there is a natural relation between the symbol and the idea it represents.

As observed by Swami Vivekananda:

"Certain symbols are universally prevalent. Many of you may think that the cross first came into existence as a symbol in connection with the Christian religion; but as a matter of fact it existed before Christianity was, before Moses was born, before the Vedas were given out, before there was any human record of human things. The cross may be found to have been in existence among the Aztecs and the Phoenicians; every race seems to have had the cross. Again, the symbol of the crucified Saviour, of a man crucified upon a cross, appears to have been known to almost every nation. The circle has been a great symbol throughout the world.

"Then there is the most universal of all symbols, the swastika. At one time it was thought that the Buddhists carried it all over the world with them, but it has been found out that ages before Buddhism it was used among nations. In old Babylon and in Egypt it was to be found. What does this show? All these symbols could not have been purely conventional. There must be some reason for them, some natural association between them and the human mind."[1]

Besides the visual symbols in concrete forms all religions have audible symbols, the names of God, representing various ideas and aspects of the Divinity. The relation between God and His name is also natural. Each name has the potency to awaken within the mind the corresponding God-consciousness.

The use of symbols, visual and audible, is not confined to religion. It is prevalent in all spheres of human life. A symbol is an emblem of something other than itself. This may be an abstract idea, a process, or a concrete object. Blind people must depend on audible symbols, the deaf on visual symbols. In most countries the flag is the symbol of nationality and of victory, the crown is the symbol of sovereignty, the scepter of rulership, and the sword of punitive justice.

The human mind naturally accepts light as symbolic of knowledge and joy, and darkness as symbolic of ignorance and sorrow. White is generally used as a mark of purity, red of passion and love, green of peace, black of mourning. The dove symbolizes an advocate of peace and the hawk an advocate of war not without reason. The use of similar

[1]*Karma-Yoga,* Chapter V, C.W. Vol. I, p. 71.

symbols among divergent races and nations of the world testifies to some natural resemblance between the symbol and what it signifies.

The widest application of symbol is the human language. Every word is symbolic; written or spoken it has a meaning. It can represent a concrete object and an abstract idea as well, or only an abstract idea, or an action. Common nouns, such as tree, man, place, represent both concrete objects and inner ideas. Abstract nouns, such as kindness, love, heroism, represent quality. Verbs, such as speak, make, and dwell, represent action.

The word *tree* represents the object *tree* and also the concept *tree*. It is applicable to each member of the tree class. It also signifies the tree class as a whole. With the perception of a tree there is the percept, that is, the impression on the mind of this particular tree; at the same time the perceiver has the concept or the general notion of the tree class. The word *tree* refers not to the percept but to the concept. This is why by knowing a single tree as a tree a child can recognize any other member of the tree class as a tree.

Similarly, the word *man* stands for every individual man and for mankind as well. It also conveys the concept of *man* to the student. Consequently, by knowing a single human being as a man one can recognize any individual of the species as a man.

The relation between the word and the concept is natural. It cannot be said to be arbitrary or conventional. It is not determined by a general agreement among certain human beings. There are, of course, technical terms, which can be regarded as purely conventional. In this context I am not concerned with them but with the words that naturally exist in the human language. A word may have several meanings, yet its relationship with each of these is natural. For example, a person may have several children, yet his relationship with each child is natural. The human language has developed as a natural process with the development of the human race.

Man feels the necessity of apprehending the abstract through the concrete. A concrete representation of an abstract idea makes the abstract clear and vivid to him. A pictorial presentation of devotional worship makes devotion real to him. Furthermore, man feels an urge to give expression to his inner ideas and sentiments in realistic terms. At the same time he finds satisfaction in doing so.

Apart from necessity this human tendency of self-expression is responsible for the development of the fine arts such as architecture, sculpture, painting, music, and poetry. It is the function of art to give concrete shape to inner ideas and ideals. All genuine arts are symbolic. They come under two main forms of symbolic expression — visual and audible. Architecture, sculpture, and painting can be counted as visual; music and poetry as audible.

Art is more or less interpretative rather than representative. In presenting a landscape a painter gives more than just a copy of the natural scenery. He gives his own view of that particular phase of nature. True art consists in the idealization, and not in the imitation, of the real. It is pleasing and uplifting. It aims to create beauty rather than provide for utility.

Religion deals primarily with suprasensible truths. So in the religious life of man there has been an imperative need for symbols, both visual and audible. In every religion there are symbolic presentations of spiritual truths. In order to comprehend the Supreme Being clearly, to worship Him with devotion and joy, to feel His presence vividly and closely, the religious spirit of man has revealed itself in all kinds of art.

But not all the fine arts have been prevalent in every religion. For instance, in Islam iconography and music are conspicuous in their absence. In Christianity dancing has not grown as an expression of religious sentiment. In Hinduism, however, all the avenues of art have been sought in approaching God.

In the development of art, religion has played a distinctive role. Perhaps all the fine arts owe their origin to religion. Some of the world's masterpieces of architecture, sculpture, painting, music, and poetry belong to the domain of religion.

From ancient times every prominent religion has developed a certain architectural type for its edifices of worship, in order to distinguish them from buildings of temporal use, and thus to intensify the worshippers' spiritual understanding and feeling. The dome-shaped top of the Buddhist stupa, of the Jewish synagogue, of the Islamic mosque remind us of the canopy of heaven guarding the world below. The lofty steeple of a Hindu temple and the tapering tower of a Gothic church, pointing to the highest, remind man of the Adorable One who is above all. The didactic and aesthetic elements in religious architecture have gradually diminished in modern time with the prevalence of the utilitarian standard.

Of the two main branches of iconography — sculpture

and painting — the former has been prominent in Hinduism and Buddhism, and the latter in Christianity. Both have deeply influenced the religious lives of the adherents. Three-dimensional iconography has been extensively used in Hinduism. Figures carved out of stone or wood, or formed by fashioning plastic material, such as clay, or shaped by casting bronze and other metals in molds — all these have served as appropriate symbols for worshipping the Divine Being in different aspects. They are varied and meaningful.

Paintings and photographs, too, have their due places in the ceremonial worship of God. Whatever symbol the worshipper may adopt, he has to contemplate its inner meaning, that is, the particular aspect of the Divinity it represents. In this way the icon becomes a great source of inspiration.

Among the icons, the likenesses of God-men are the most impressive and animating. The great spiritual leaders who are known as Divine Incarnations, or the Messengers of God, or as the Prophets, who are adored as the Saviours of souls by their respective followers, are the most remarkable manifestations of the Divinity in human form. They live in constant God-consciousness and thus make God real to us.

We can conceive of God through speculative reason or through scriptural study, but cannot be free from doubts as to His existence or His real nature until we know God-like personages and hear their version of direct experience. It is through them that we can understand what Divine love, Divine power, Divine purity, Divine wisdom, Divine joy really mean, because they demonstrate these attributes in their lives. They represent God to us more than any celestial being can.

We cannot worship God except through them. Their lives manifest man's love for God on the one hand, and God's love for man on the other. Through these great ones we receive Divine grace and compassion. At the same time they live as ideal lovers of God. All the virtues of a spiritual aspirant are evident in them. They are the most illustrious exemplars of their own teachings. Their images prove to be natural symbols for the worship of the Divinity, and serve as sources of inspiration for spiritual aspirants, particularly in the early stages of development.

How does the worship of an image lead to the realization of God? It is not that the very image is worshipped. It is the Divinity represented by it or the Divine glory radiated by it that is worshipped. Only the appreciative mind can receive inspiration from an image. The worshipper does not look upon it as a mere image, but as the emblem of Divine purity, Divine wisdom, Divine love, Divine freedom, Divine joy. In thinking of it he thinks of the ideal that it evokes.

As observed by Sri Ramakrishna, just as an artificial apple reminds one of the real apple, so does a representation of God remind one of God. The concrete image helps the votary to concentrate the mind on the spiritual reality symbolized by the form. Through the form he reaches the Formless. As a result he feels the presence of the Omnipresent Being in one form at least.

On seeing the portrait of an illustrious man you feel uplifted. It is because you see the picture not as a mere picture, but as the personification of the ideal he stood for, as an embodiment of the principles he exemplified. Similarly, the worshipper looks upon the image as the representation of the Divine Being. With regard to the image of the Divine Mother, Kali, Sri Ramakrishna remarked: "This is not just a clay image or a stone image, but the very embodiment of Divine Consciousness. That is what the image stands for." It so happens that through the worshipper's faith and devotion, the stone image becomes infused with life, so to speak. The worshipper feels the living presence of the Omnipresent Being emanating from there.

At whatever time, and by whatever method you worship God — physical, verbal, or mental — your mind turns to Him. It comes in touch with the Holiest of the Holy, imperceptible though the contact may be. Even the least thought of Him, who is Pure Spirit, Supreme Consciousness, is conducive to the purification of the mind. From the purification of the mind proceeds clarity of vision. You develop the power to comprehend the spiritual reality. You become convinced of the existence of Divine Being as the all-pervading Self shining within each individual as the inmost Self, as the Soul of souls. It is then that your whole mind turns to Him with loving devotion. You see the image as the vivid representation of the Divine Being, and approach it with piety and veneration.

It is useless, even presumptuous, to judge the relative importance of the images, their superiority and inferiority. The aspirant has to select the one that is most meaningful to him, the one that evokes his utmost faith and devotion. Through the chosen one he should persistently worship the Lord with all earnestness. Gradually he will derive the full benefit of the worship. The truth about God will be revealed to him. He will feel the Divine presence within and without. Says Sri Krishna, the Divine Incarnation:

Among the images and other icons, a person may worship Me just in that in which he may have faith at the time. For I am the Self of all and dwell in everything as well as in his own self.

(S.B. XI:27.48)

Seated before the image the worshipper meditates on the Supreme Being with the eyes closed, knowing Him to be the indwelling Self. He tries to visualize within his mind the likeness of the concrete image outside as clearly as possible. He fixes his thoughts on the mental image while meditating on its meaning. Through deep meditation his mind becomes absorbed in the Spiritual Reality represented by the form. Through the form he attains the formless, the indwelling Self behind the form. He finds himself united with That. Like light united with Light, the individual consciousness becomes united with Supreme Consciousness, the all-pervading Self. Thus he becomes completely free from the bondage of relative existence.

Sri Krishna thus sums up the result of the practice of meditation on His concrete image:

With one's mind thus absorbed, one sees Me alone in oneself and sees oneself united to Me, the Self of all, like light united to light.

A spiritual aspirant who thus concentrates his mind through intense meditation will soon blow out the delusion about sense-objects, finite knowledge, and action [which constitute the phenomenal order].

(S.B. XI:14.45,46)

But the devotee need not depend solely on self-effort. Divine grace helps him. As the worshipper approaches God with intense longing for His vision, so does God come forward to remove the veil of darkness from within his heart. As declared by Sri Krishna in the *Bhagavad-gita:*

> I am the origin of all. From Me all things proceed. Knowing this the wise worship Me with loving devotion.
>
> With their thoughts directed to Me, with their lives dedicated to Me, enlightening one another and talking about Me constantly they are contented and rejoice.
>
> On those who are ever devoted to Me and worship Me with love I bestow the concentration of buddhi [the determinative mind] by which they attain Me.
>
> Out of compassion for such as these I, dwelling in their hearts, dispel with the shining lamp of knowledge the darkness born of ignorance.   (B.G. X:8-11)

Like the visual symbols the verbal symbols have proved very helpful in man's spiritual life. They are extensively used in all religions. Prayer is the universal verbal approach to God. It is prevalent in all theistic religions. In a very restricted sense prayer means supplication for a desired object. But in a wide sense it includes such verbal modes of worship as chanting hymns, singing devotional songs, offering salutations, and repeated utterance of a sacred word or formula.

Usually a prayer consists of many words. But as the worshipper's understanding of the spiritual ideal grows deeper and his devotion to God intensifies, just a few words fraught with meaning are enough to convey his fervent thoughts and feelings. His mind becomes focused on one or two ideas. He feels assured that all that he needs is the grace of God, or devotion to Him, or complete self-resignation to His will. Then his prayer takes such condensed forms as —

"Have mercy on me, O Lord"; "Grant me, O Lord, devotion to Thy blessed feet"; "To Thee I surrender myself"; "Thou art my all in all"; "I seek refuge in Thee and Thee alone." With all earnestness he repeatedly says the same prayer.

Similarly, when the spiritual aspirant understands the true import of a great religious leader's life and message, the very name stirs up his adoration and serves as a source of inspiration for him. Each time he utters the name he feels uplifted. It proves to be a potent force to transform him.

A significant epithet of God, e.g., "The Adorable One"; "The Supreme Beloved"; "The All-wise"; "The All-merciful"; "The Soul of all souls"; is like the potent seed of God-consciousness. In Sanskrit there are innumerable words expressive of different attributes and aspects of the Divinity. Being repeatedly uttered with understanding, faith, and devotion any one of them serves to awaken the corresponding God-consciousness in the adorer. As observed by Sri Ramakrishna, "There is great power in the seed of God's name. It destroys ignorance. A seed is tender, and the sprout soft; still it pierces the hard ground. The ground breaks and makes way for the sprout."[2]

There are several ways of purifying the mind, such as moral observances, charitable deeds, austerities, association with the holy, right performance of duties, and ceremonial worship. But none of these is as efficacious as the repetition of a significant name of God along with meditation on its meaning. Other methods can purge the conscious levels of the mind, but they cannot penetrate the subconscious region, where the impressions of past deeds and experiences

[2] *The Gospel of Sri Ramakrishna,* trans. by Swami Nikhilananda, p.210. Ramakrishna-Vivekananda Center, New York: 1942.

are imbedded and where the wrong tendencies and desires are rooted.

For cleaning different things, e.g., glass, wood, linen, wool, we adopt different processes. For cleaning the human mind there is also a special process. It is the repeated utterance of a sacred word or formula while contemplating its meaning. The repetition can be audible, semi-audible, or mental. Mental repetition is the most effective of the three ways. This verbal mode of worship is prevalent in other religions as well — such as Buddhism, Christianity, and Islam. In some cases a rosary is used. The worshipper repeats the word-symbol while counting the beads.

In my early youth in India, one evening many years ago I met a Sufi saint, who was living in a house-boat close to a city. I saw him seated on a carpet, in the dim light of a kerosene lamp, holding a long rosary of crystal beads in his hands. He was counting the beads while mentally repeating a sacred formula. After some preliminary talk I asked him why he had been doing this. "There is a special kind of soap for cleaning the human mind. I am applying this soap to my mind," he replied.

If you find a nugget of gold you can remove whatever impurities there may be on its surface by such methods as dusting, washing, or polishing. But you cannot purify the nugget of any adulteration except by the process of smelting. Similarly, the only way to cure the mind of its ingrained vices is the penetration of the Divine Light.

In the Vedic religion there are mystic words or syllables, which are counted as veritable seeds of spiritual consciousness (vija-mantras). The most comprehensive of them all is the syllable "Om," which stands for both Saguna and

Nirguna Brahman (God immanent and God transcendent). Besides this, there are other seed-words signifying God's love, power, or wisdom. A mystic syllable or two are usually added to the prevalent sacred word or formula to enhance its potency. The mystic syllables are also used singly or jointly for the purpose of repetition.

A word-symbol suited to the worshipper's inner nature is prescribed for repetition as an aid to the practice of meditation. Persistent, systematic repetition (with or without a rosary) purifies the worshipper's mind, develops his spiritual insight and intensifies his devotion to God and the longing for His vision.

In his *Yoga Aphorisms* Pantanjali refers to the mystic syllable "Om" as helpful to meditation and God-realization (see p. 199). In the words of Swami Vivekananda:

"Even as in the case of the least differentiated and the most universal symbol Om, thought and sound-symbol are seen to be inseparably associated with each other, so also this law of their inseparable association applies to the many differentiated views of God and the universe; each of them therefore must have a particular word-symbol to express it. These word-symbols, evolved out of the deepest spiritual perceptions of sages, symbolize and express as nearly as possible the particular view of God and the universe they stand for. And as the Om represents the Akhanda, the undifferentiated Brahman, the others represent the Khanda or the differentiated views of the same Being; and they are all helpful to divine meditation and the acquisition of true knowledge."[3]

[3] *Bhakti-Yoga*, chap. on "The Mantra, Om: Word and Wisdom." C.W. Vol. III, pp. 58-59.

CHAPTER V

Prayer and Meditation

Prayer is preparatory to meditation. It is through meditation that one realizes God. In deep meditation when the mind becomes completely absorbed in God, the one Self of all, then His light shines in the mind, removes all darkness, removes the veil of ignorance (ajnana), and the Supreme Being becomes Self-revealed. When you see God directly, you find yourself in Him. In Him alone is eternal life, in Him alone is complete freedom from all bondages and sufferings, in Him alone is supreme beatitude. Says Jesus Christ, "Blessed are the pure in heart for they shall see God." One condition for seeing God is purity of heart; and those who see God, attain supreme beatitude. Therefore they are blessed.

As declared by the *Mundaka Upanishad:*

> When He who is immanent and transcendent is perceived, directly experienced, then all doubts are dispelled. All knots of the heart that tie an individual to this sensible universe are completely cut asunder, and all the deposit of [past] karma is wiped out.
>
> (Mu.U. II:2.8)

Complete freedom is attained through the perception

of God. It is the highest objective of life and the direct way to this is meditation. All other spiritual courses are preparatory to the practice of meditation.

Indeed, different modes of worship are intended to prepare the mind for the practice of meditation by generating devotion within. Prayer is the simplest method of worship by which the mind is prepared for the practice of meditation.

You can also convert your secular deeds into a mode of worship by doing your duty with complete self-resignation — by surrendering the ego in the form of "I-ness" and "my-ness" to God. Such performance of duty also becomes a spiritual practice, turns the mind Godward, and prepares the mind gradually for the practice of meditation.

Besides the faithful performance of duty with dispassion there are other physical methods by which you can approach God. For instance, you may serve a temple or a holy person; you may associate with a saint; you may make a pilgrimage; you may offer something you like, such as flowers, light, incense, or food, to the altar in the name of the Lord; you may bow down to the Lord — all these physical courses prepare the mind for the practice of meditation by generating devotion to God within.

Then there are verbal courses. You may say prayers to the Supreme Being, chant his praise or sing devotional songs, or read scriptures or listen to the exposition of scriptures. Any such verbal practice or mental operation (e.g., remembering God or contemplating on God as far as possible), prepares the mind for the practice of meditation.

How is this effected? Each time you perform any worship in the name of the Lord it tends to generate devotion within your heart, because it turns your mind toward God; you contact God, slight though it may be. He is the Holiest of the Holy. If you contact worldly people, you will tend to acquire worldliness. If you contact the pure-minded, you will acquire purity of mind to some extent.

When you contemplate on God your mind becomes more or less concentrated on Him. As the mind is purified by contact with the Holiest of the Holy, devotion grows within. So each and every form of worship helps you to fix the mind on God, attain inner purification and also acquire devotion. Even if you are not capable of fixing the mind fully, whatever you do in the name of the Lord, even the slightest remembrance of Him, helps you. In this way each and every act of worship prepares the mind for the practice of meditation by purifying the mind, and also by developing devotion to the Lord within.

You cannot meditate on God simply by knowing the technique of meditation. It is not so easy. The principal factor that enables the mind to be concentrated on God is devotion to the Lord. It is a simple truth in this world that you meditate on what you like or love. If you love your dog you will meditate more or less on the dog. If you love your house you will meditate more or less on the house; if a wife loves her husband intensely she will meditate on the husband more than anything else. If the husband loves the wife he will necessarily meditate on her most of the time. This is the simple truth.

In spiritual life, also, the same principle holds good. You cannot concentrate your mind on God as long as the mind is filled with all kinds of worldly thoughts and feelings and sense desires. The point is, do you really want God? You cannot attain love for God just by a trick. You have to continue the proper method of worship that is suitable to you. The different forms of worship mentioned above prepare the mind for the practice of concentration by purifying the mind and by generating devotion within.

Prayer is evidently a verbal approach to God. You pray to God, and God responds to your prayer if the prayer is deep and earnest. You may pray to God for anything you want. Persons who are worldly-minded naturally pray to God for worldly objectives — for power, for position, for beauty, for youth, for longevity, for rescue from a calamity, for various secular interests. If the prayers are earnest then they are answered. Contrarily, persons who are spiritually inclined naturally pray to God for spiritual values.

A person cannot be spiritually-minded until he realizes the futility of worldly desires. We have explained elsewhere how a person who follows the path of virtue becomes disillusioned of all dualities. Then he understands that simply by attaining prosperity he cannot solve the problem of life. This life continues to be a drama of birth, growth, decay, and death. One is inevitably subject to the dual experience of pain and pleasure, of love and hate, of hope and fear, of success and failure. This dual experience is his lot whether he lives in a civilized society or a barbarous community, whether he lives in a royal palace or in a farmer's cottage. He cannot avoid this dual experience. This is the common lot of a human being which does not change.

In spite of all technological inventions, in spite of varieties of scientific discoveries, in spite of all political strategies, in spite of all utilitarian devices, the basic experience of man, the common background of humanity does not change. What is the common background? The drama of birth, growth, decay, and death. This drama of smiles and tears, of hope and fear, of rise and fall still continues. All changes are on the surface. So this experience has to be changed if we want to solve the problem of life effectively. More problems are often created than solved by inventing something for the sake of pleasure and comfort. The problems continue because we live in the world of dualities, of pairs of opposites.

When a person is disillusioned of dualities he wants to go beyond all relativity. He wants to reach that Reality which is absolute. God alone is good in the absolute sense. Nothing else is good in the absolute sense. He alone is all-good. Unless a person is convinced of this his mind does not turn towards God in the true sense. He cannot be a spiritual aspirant — a seeker of God.

When a person understands this truth and recognizes the limitation of all secular values, he develops the insight that the one supreme purpose of life is to realize God, to see God. It is then that he seeks God as an ideal, as a Goal. Then he does not pray to God for secular interests. He prays to God for spiritual values. He realizes that it is spiritual treasures only that do not rot, that do not rust, that no thief can steal.

No longer does he pray for secular interests. If he ever prays to God for secular interests it is for the sake of his spiritual development. For instance, he may pray to God for good health and a secure position for the sake of spiritual benefit. He understands that to pray to God for secular values — power, wealth, beauty, position and so forth — is like collecting pebbles after going to a mine of diamonds. It is like allaying one's thirst by drinking ditch water after reaching a perennial spring of ambrosia. Who but a child will ever approach the emperor of emperors for toys and dolls?

It is to be understood that this life ever continues to be the drama of smiles and tears, of hopes and fears, of success and failure, wherever a person may be. It was so in the past, it is so in the present; it is so in the East, it is so in the West. You cannot get out of this maze. Those who recognize the limitation of the dual experience, the limitation of the relative order, they seek God as an ideal, as a goal. Without right understanding this is not possible.

The Vedic seers recognized the importance of right understanding. In the *Svetasvatara Upanishad* we find the following prayers:

> May He, the Lord of the universe, the great Seer, the Terror of the Terrible, Who is the origin of the gods and their Sustainer, Who brought into being the Cosmic Soul in the beginning, may He grant us salutary understanding.
>
> (III:4)

> May that Self-effulgent Being, who, though one and undiversified, gives rise to diversities by His manifold powers, without any motive of His own, who at the end [of the cycle] withdraws unto Himself the universe, may He endow us with salutary understanding.
>
> (IV:1)

Right understanding is much more valuable than all our external resources. You cannot utilize your external or your internal resources for your own benefit unless you have right understanding, unless you have wisdom. The Vedantic sages understood this, that more than anything else the one thing man needs is right understanding. But for this he will not be able to utilize his wealth properly. He will not be able to utilize his friends properly, he will not be able to utilize his position properly, his belongings properly, he may even use them wrongly for his own harm. Even his intelligence, his aesthetic abilities he will not be able to utilize properly without right understanding.

So the first thing we need is true understanding, true wisdom. And then, whatever we get we can use for our own benefit. Otherwise, the acquisition of power and position will not help us. So there can be many different forms of prayer a person can adopt for lack of true understanding.

In the beginning a seeker of God may use many words in his prayer; but as his understanding becomes clearer, as his spiritual feeling deepens and his faith becomes intense, he realizes that all that he needs is devotion to God. So he prays to God only for devotion. He simply says, "O Lord, may I have true love for Thee! May I have devotion to Thee. Wholehearted devotion is all that I need." The prayers become shorter, the devotee does not use too many words.

He recognizes at the same time that without the purification of the heart devotion does not grow within, that all he needs is God's mercy, so he prays to God just for the purification of the heart. Then he prays, "O Lord, have mercy on me, have mercy on me, forgive my weaknesses." That becomes his sole prayer. In this way as his spiritual feeling deepens, his prayers become shorter. He also realizes that without God's grace devotion does not grow within, so he prays to God just for His grace, just for the development of love for Him within. Such a prayer becomes the keynote of his life.

It is to be noted that prayer does not necessarily mean asking God for something. In a restricted sense prayer means that. But in a wide sense, prayer means a verbal approach to God. You may chant the glory of God; it arouses devotional feeling within you. This is also a prayer. You may sing devotional songs without asking for anything. They are also prayers. So, any verbal approach to God is a prayer. You may say, "Thou art my Mother, Thou art my Father, Thou art my Friend, Thou art my Companion, Thou art my Knowledge, Thou art my Treasure, Thou art my All-in-all, O God of gods!" without begging for anything.

Or you may simply say, "I bow down to Thee, O Lord. I bow down to Thee, O Lord." For example:

> I bow down to the Self-effulgent Being, who has pervaded the whole universe, who is in fire, who is in water, who is in the plants, who is in the trees.
>
> (Sv.U. II:17)
>
> I bow to Thee, O Thou Pure Existence, the one Support of all the worlds;
> I bow to Thee, O Thou Pure Intelligence, the one Self of the multiform universe;
> I bow to Thee, the Nondual Being, the Giver of Freedom.
> I bow to Thee, Supreme Brahman, Limitless and Absolute.
>
> (Ma.T. I)

Then there are optative prayers:

> May my speech be engaged in the narration of Thy attributes; may my ears be engaged in hearing about

Thee; may my hands be occupied with the performance of
Thy deeds; may my mind ever remember Thee; may my
eyes constantly see the holy persons, Thy embodiments;
may my head be engaged in bowing down to this universe,
Thy abode. (S.B. X:10.38)

May all go beyond misery, may all attain well-being,
may all gain right knowledge, may all rejoice in all places.
(anon.)

Any prayer that helps to set your heart on God will lead
to the purification of the mind and the development of
devotion within.

It is held by the Vedantic teachers that the cultivation of
devotion to God means but the manifestation of devotion
that is already within man. The devotion that he is seeking is
already in him. Man is a born lover of God, a born seeker of
God. Knowingly or unknowingly, rightly or wrongly, he is
seeking the Highest, he is seeking the Best. In the long run he
understands that his search for the lovable will end only
when he will find the supreme object of love, the Highest, the
Best, who is only One. There cannot be two bests or two
highests. Hundreds of high, hundreds of higher there can be;
hundreds of good, hundreds of better there can be; but the
Highest, the Best is One; and this is the quest of human life,
to find the Highest, to find the Best. We are trying here and
there, everywhere, to discover that.

So a devotee says, "In this world, O Lord, in search of
wealth, I have found Thee the greatest Treasure. In this
world, O Lord, in search of someone to love I have found
Thee the most lovable one. Where else but at Thy blessed
feet shall I seek refuge! Thou art my Goal, my Abode, my

All-in-All!" We are in search of the true object of love, the Highest and Best. After swallowing many sweet and bitter pills in the journey of life, at last the seeker comes to the understanding that this search for the lovable will end only when he finds the Supreme object of love, the perfect One. The human heart is meant for the Highest and Best. Man cannot stop short anywhere else.

With this insight our spiritual feeling deepens, our search for God becomes intensified, our prayers become concentrated. One or two ideas become the keynote of spiritual life. I shall quote one prayer from Sri Ramakrishna, how intensely he prayed to the Divine Mother with childlike simplicity. If you have devotion then only is it possible for you to meditate on God. And through deep meditation you can see God, and when you see God you find yourself in God. He is the very perfection of existence.

Addressing the Divine Mother Sri Ramakrishna said:

"O Mother, I throw myself on Thy mercy; I take shelter at Thy Hallowed Feet. I do not want bodily comforts; I do not crave name and fame; I do not seek the eight occult powers. Be gracious and grant that I may have pure love for Thee, a love unsmitten by desire, untainted by any selfish ends — a love craved by the devotee for the sake of love alone.

"And grant me the favour, O Mother, that I may not be deluded by Thy world-bewitching maya, that I may never be attached to the world, to 'woman and gold,' conjured up by Thy inscrutable maya! O Mother, there is no one but Thee whom I may call my own. Mother, I do not know how to worship; I am without austerity; I have neither devotion nor knowledge. Be gracious, Mother, and out of Thy infinite mercy grant me love for Thy Lotus Feet."[1]

As a person continues to pray to God intensely one or two ideas become the keynote of his spiritual life. Then the prayer becomes short such as, "Grant me love for Thee, grant me love for Thee." Just one or two ideas he holds to continuously. Later one or two words become sufficient and most meaningful in his spiritual life. He says repeatedly a prayer such as "Have mercy on me"; "Be gracious unto me"; "Grant me devotion to Thy Blessed Feet"; "May I see Thee." Sri Ramakrishna says God's name is the potent seed of spiritual consciousness. If a person repeats the name of God, his body, senses, and mind become pure.

In case you understand the true significance of the life of Jesus Christ and have devotion to Him, just the word *Jesus* will be enough for you. You will not have to say or hear too many things with regard to Him. Each time you utter His name you will be overwhelmed with devotion to Him, with love for Him. Similarly if a person understands the true significance of the life and teachings of Krishna, then the word *Krishna* will be enough for him. The word *Krishna* will give rise to all the spiritual thoughts and feelings connected with the spiritual understanding.

Just as each and every water course is winding its way toward the ocean, so every human soul is winding its way towards God, the great center of attraction of all. For one who has understood the exemplary life of Rama and the

[1]*Gospel*, p.731.

meaning of the word *Rama*, just the word *Rama* will be enough for him. So in this way just a single word indicative of Divinity becomes the focal point of one's spiritual life. Then the person continuously repeats that name. That name works in the subsoil of the mind, purifying the mind from the bottom.

Our weaknesses do not wholly dwell in the surface of the mind. The majority of our weaknesses dwell in the subsoil of the mind so that has to be cleansed. For this purpose the repetition of a single word signifying the Lord, the Holiest of the Holy, is most fruitful. There is no specific other than the potent name of God which can purify the bottom of the mind as efficaciously.

Besides the potent name of God there are some seed words in Hindu spiritual culture which germinate Divine love, power, wisdom, and so forth, being repeatedly uttered with devotion after one knows their meaning.

Every word is a form of inner consciousness. The word *love* is not just l-o-v-e, a combination of four letters, it is something deep. The word *tree* is not just something which you see before your eyes or the sound that you hear with your ears, but something much deeper, so these words being heard or spoken awaken that inner consciousness once you know their meaning. As you understand the true meaning of God or Jesus or Krishna or Rama or Ramakrishna, the very utterance of any of these words will awaken that inner consciousness.

Consequently if any of these words are repeated persistently with some faith and devotion, they purify the mind from the very bottom and develop love for God. Sri Krishna gives an illustration. Suppose a lump of gold is brought to you. Now, you want to purify it. If you note any dust on it you wipe it off. Then you may notice some mark of clay or something else embedded in it, so now you must smelt it, and for this you will have to go to an expert — a goldsmith who will put the lump of gold into fire and separate the alloy from the pure gold.[2]

Similarly, Sri Krishna says, "The potent name of God serves this purpose." Simply by moral observance, by association with the righteous people, by right deeds, you can clear the surface of the mind but unless the potent name of God is instilled into your mind by an expert teacher, the impurities that are embedded within the subsoil of the mind cannot be removed. And unless these are removed, deep seated sense desires will always remain. True devotion to God will not grow within you. So, according to Hindu spiritual culture, a person should repeat the name of the Lord, and gradually his mind will be further purified and true devotion will grow.

The repetition of the word, which is the concentrated form of prayer, is linked with meditation. As you repeat the word or the formula, you meditate on the form of God — the form through which you think of God or worship Him. It is very difficult for us to think of God without a concrete form. God is the finest, the subtlest of all existences. The mind fails to comprehend Him. It is said in one of the Upanishads,

> That Supreme Being cannot be seen with the eyes. Nor words can express Him. Indeed, none of the senses can actually perceive Him. He cannot be reached by the performance of deeds or the practice of austerities. Hands

[2]S.B. XI:14.25.

cannot grasp Him. Mind fails to comprehend Him. When
the mind is purified through the clarity of understanding,
then the aspirant realizes Him, the partless One, through
deep meditation.

(Mu.U. III:1.8)

As you repeat the word, you meditate on the form
corresponding to the word you have chosen. Word and form
go together in practice. If you repeat the words *Jesus Christ*
you also visualize the form of Jesus Christ. In case you
repeat the word *Krishna*, you will also see the form of
Krishna. God is essentially beyond form. There is no
question about it. But we cannot reach the impersonal, the
formless One but through form. So, the spiritual aspirants
have to choose some form and corresponding to that form
there should be some word. If these two are combined, then
the mind becomes purified effectively and spontaneous
longing for God grows.

You see, spontaneous longing is necessary, not
calculating devotion; natural ardent devotion is necessary
— then one can meditate on God. When he can meditate on
God, the One Self of all, as his innermost self, then he can
realize Him as the mind is completely absorbed in Him.

CHAPTER VI

Karma-Yoga as Preparatory to the Practice of Meditation

Meditation is the final spiritual course for realizing God. Until the mind is quite absorbed in Him, He is not revealed. Without going through subsidiary courses one cannot meditate on God effectively. The purpose of these courses is to gradually remove from the mind all attachment to the transitory and develop the capacity for consecration to the Eternal One.

Whoever has faith in God can try to practice meditation on Him in his own way at any stage of development, but until his mind is freed from all distractions and wholly concentrated on God, he will not be able to perceive Him.

Sri Ramakrishna says, "The thread does not pass through the eye of the needle as long as a single fibre is sticking out of it."

It is said that once a certain yogi was so deeply absorbed in meditation that even though a bird sat on his head he was unaware of it.

As regards the gradation of the preparatory courses, we have explained elsewhere that it is through the long practice of virtue that the human mind recognizes the futility of all that is transitory, and looks far beyond to the Eternal.

Even for moral development without which practice of virtue is not possible, Hindu teachers have followed the graded course of training. In the *Brihadaranyaka Upanishad*[1] we find the following story.

Three types of human beings, some of godly nature, some of human nature, and some of devilish nature, went to a teacher for instruction. The teacher told them to live with him for a number of years. His purpose was to uplift them by his exemplary way of living. There is a common saying, "Example is better than precept." Instruction does not help the pupil as much as the influence of an exemplary life does. In ancient India specially for this reason the students lived in close touch with the teacher. After these three types of students had lived with the teacher for some time they came forward for instruction.

The first type of students, who were of godly nature, approached the teacher, "Be gracious to give us instruction, sir," they said.

The teacher simply uttered the syllable "Da," the first Sanskrit letter of the instruction. Then he asked, "Do you understand?"

"Yes, sir," said the students. "You mean 'Damayata (practice self-control).' "

"Yes, this is the instruction," replied the teacher.

Next the second type of students, who were of human nature, approached the teacher. The teacher uttered the same syllable, "Da," and said, "This is the instruction." "Do you understand?" he further asked.

The students said, "Yes, sir, you mean 'Datta (be

[1] V:2.1-3.

charitable).' "

"Yes, this is the instruction," said the teacher.

Then the third type of human beings, who were of devilish nature, came forward. "Instruction, sir," they said.

Then the teacher uttered the same syllable, "Da." "This is the instruction. Do you understand?"

"Yes, sir, you mean 'Dayadhvam (be kind),' " replied the students.

"Yes, this is the instruction," said the teacher.

Those who were of devilish nature were given the instruction "Be kind; that is, don't hurt anybody. Be non-violent." Just this much they were expected to practice.

The second type of students, who were relatively higher in nature, were given the instruction, "Datta (be charitable)." It was a positive course.

The first type of human beings were given the instruction of self-control. This means inner purification by the practice of virtue; that is, the development of such moral qualities as compassion, sympathy, love, humility, tolerance, while subjugating vices such as anger, jealousy, hatred, pride, and intolerance.

To earn money by fair or foul means and give for charitable purposes is not so difficult, but to develop virtues while controlling vice is hard to practice. This requires self-mastery.

Thus, in giving moral and spiritual instruction the Hindu teachers have followed the principle of giving instruction suited to the inner development of the student. They hold the view that even from the lowest level of life a person can reach the highest level by following a graded course according to his stage of development. This method is known as "The Doctrine of differentiation of the grades of the spiritual aspirants (for imparting instruction)."

As we have already mentioned, it is through the continued practice of virtue that the human mind recognizes the futility of all that is transitory, howsoever great, howsoever small, and looks far beyond to the Eternal One. But the mind subject to old habits cannot easily turn away from its wonted course. It has the inveterate tendency to move along the old ruts. It is said that habit forms second nature; we know the wrong, we condemn it, yet the wrong we pursue. The purpose of Karma-yoga is to make the mind free from these inveterate tendencies. Thus purified the mind develops an inwardness. It is set firmly on the spiritual path, on the direct way to God-realization.

Karma-yoga means work performed as yoga, that is, as a method of God-realization. It is a spiritual discipline. It is preparatory to Bhakti-yoga and also to Jnana-yoga. Bhakti-yoga is the direct way to the realization of Saguna Brahman. Jnana-yoga is the direct way to the realization of Nirguna Brahman. Being preparatory to either of these yogas, Karma-yoga is the indirect way to the realization of God.

It is understood that one cannot practice Karma-yoga until the mind recognizes the futility of transitory pleasures and possessions, develops dispassion and accepts the Eternal One, the Supreme Being as the Goal, as the Ideal. It is He who transcends all that is transitory, all that is finite. The mere performance of unselfish work or humanitarian deeds cannot be counted as the practice of Karma-yoga.

One essential condition for the practice of Karma-yoga subsidiary to Bhakti-yoga, is that the aspirant should make it a point to do the work as an offering to the Lord by giving up all claim to the work done and its result. In order to dedicate work to God, the doer must be free from twofold egoism: "I am the doer, therefore the result of the work is mine." A Karma-yogi naturally does good deeds, because nobody can be a Karma-yogi until he is established in the path of virtue. But in this world of dualities good and evil cannot be completely dissociated. There is nothing wholly good, there is nothing wholly evil. It depends on our standard of judgment.

A Karma-yogi who dedicates all work to the Lord is not affected any more by its consequences, good or evil. So says Sri Krishna in the *Bhagavad-gita:*

> He who performs work resigning it to God, giving up all attachment is not tainted by the results of the work, just as a lotus leaf is not moistened by water [though it grows in water].
>
> The followers of Karma-yoga perform work, giving up all attachment [being free from egoism], solely with the body, the mind, the intellect, and the organs, for self-purification.   (B.G. V:10,11)

Sri Krishna urges Arjuna to make an offering of all work to Him.

> Whatever thou doest, whatever thou eatest, whatever thou bestowest in sacrifice, whatever thou givest away, whatever austerity thou practicest, O Son of Kunti [Arjuna], dedicate them all to me.
>
> Thus shalt thou be freed from the bondages of actions bearing good and evil results, with the heart steadfast in the yoga of renunciation, and liberated, thou shalt come unto me.   (IX:27,28)

The self-same principle of the dedication of all work to the Lord has been urged in the *Srimad Bhagavatam:*

> Whatever a person does with the body, with the organ of speech, by the senses, by the mind [deliberative mind], by intellect [the determinitive mind], by egoism, or due to natural tendencies, should be dedicated to the Supreme Being.
>
> (S.B. XI:2.36)

One cannot retire from the active life without the practice of Karma-yoga. So says Sri Krishna:

> But renunciation of action, O mighty armed [Arjuna], is difficult to attain without performance of selfless action. The sage devoted to selfless action attains Brahman before long.
>
> (B.G. V:6)

In the *Srimad Bhagavatam* Sri Krishna says to Uddhava:

> Karma-yoga is to be practiced until the mind is dispassionate, until there develops spontaneous interest in hearing about Me.
>
> (S.B. XI:20.9)

Since a Karma-yogi is unperturbed by success and failure he attains equanimity of mind, which, being habitual, paves the way for the practice of meditation.

Sri Krishna urges Arjuna to practice this equanimity even in the battlefield. Arjuna belonged to the ruling class. It was his duty to maintain justice, to establish peace and order by the subjugation of the wicked and the protection of the virtuous.

> [Being a Karma-yogi] it is your duty to work without claiming the fruits of the work. Be thou not subject to the fruits of actions nor should you have attraction for inaction.
>
> Being steadfast in yoga [karma-yoga], O Dhananjaya [Arjuna], perform actions, abandoning attachment, unperturbed by success and failure. This evenness of mind is yoga.
>
> Work [with desire] is verily far inferior to that performed with the mind unperturbed with the thoughts of results, O Dhananjaya, seek refuge in this evenness of mind. Wretched are they who act for results.
>
> Imbued with the evenness of mind, one frees oneself in this life, alike from virtue and vice [their impressions embedded within]. Devote thyself therefore to this [Karma] yoga. This yoga is the secret of work.
>
> (B.G. II:47-50)

By continuing the practice of Karma-yoga subsidiary to Bhakti-yoga, as the deep-seated longing for transitory pleasures and possessions are eradicated, the mind turns more and more toward the Supreme Being, the Eternal One. The aspirant finds more and more interest in associating with the devotees of God, in reading devotional texts, in rendering service to the temple, and so forth.

Karma-yoga can be so practiced as to pave the way to Self-knowledge. It depends on the inner attitude of the worker. While working the seeker of Self-knowledge must remember that the real self of man is ever distinct from the body, the organs, and the mind, as well as from the external objects, being their cognizer. Consciousness belongs to the cognizer and not to the cognized. As their cognizer the Self is luminous, pure, free, changeless, immortal. All movements belong to the cognized and not to the cognizer.

The cognized are the transformations of the three gunas of prakriti — *sattva, rajas,* and *tamas.*[2] As he is working the seeker of Self-knowledge must remember, it is the gunas of prakriti in the form of the body, the organs, and the mind that dwell on the gunas in the form of objects. The Self is ever aloof from them.

So says Sri Krishna in the *Bhagavad-gita:*

> The gunas of Prakriti [in the form of the body, the organs and the mind] perform all actions. With the understanding deluded by egoism, a person thinks, 'I am the doer.' But one with true insight into the domains of gunas and karma, knowing that the gunas as senses merely rest on the gunas as objects, does not become attached.
>
> (III:27,28)

When a seeker of Self-knowledge attains purity of mind through Karma-yoga, he finds himself in possession of the four essential prerequisites of Jnana-yoga (sadhana-catustaya).[3] These are:

1. The discrimination between the real and the unreal, that is, firm conviction of the mind to the effect that Brahman is real and the manifold is unreal.

2. A dispassion for the enjoyment of all fruits of action here and hereafter, as a result of the understanding of their futility.

[2]See note on the gunas, p.126.
[3]See Shankara's *Viveka-chudamani,* verses 18, 19.

3. The six-fold assets, namely,
   (i) Control of the mind (shama).
   (ii) Control of the senses (dama).
   (iii) Withdrawal of the mind (uparati), i.e., the
   cessation of distractions.
   (iv) Fortitude (titiksha), i.e., being unaffected by the
   pairs of opposites.
   (v) Faith in the words of the preceptor and the
   Vedanta (sraddha).
   (vi) Concentration of the mind on Brahman
   (samadhana).

4. Yearning for Liberation or freedom from all bondages superimposed by ajnana.

That Karma-yoga prepares the way to Jnana-yoga has been aptly expressed by Sureswaracharya in his *Naiskarmyasiddhih* (Sec.48):

> Actions (free from desires) develop an inwardness of the mind by purifying it, and then their purpose being served, they disappear like the clouds after the rains.

CHAPTER VII

Preparation for Meditation in Bhakti-Yoga

Bhakti-yoga is the path of devotion. It is the direct approach to Saguna Brahman, the Supreme Being in relation to the universe constituted of the three gunas.

The Ultimate Reality, according to Vedanta, is verily "the One without a Second," beyond thought, beyond word. Mind fails to think of That, speech fails to express That, yet That is not non-entity or void, but Pure Existence, Absolute Being. Nor is That Being material entity bereft of consciousness. That Being is Consciousness Itself. That is to say, That is real to Itself. That Pure Being which is Pure Consciousness is Bliss Itself. This means That is the ideal reality, perfection itself. So the Ultimate Reality according to Vedanta is pure Being–Consciousness–Bliss (Sat-chit-ananda).[1]

That Reality, "the One without a Second," designated Nondual Brahman, is immanent in this apparent manifold. Though immanent, That is all-transcendent, not at all affected by diversities. As immanent in the universe That is Saguna, being related to the universe constituted of the three

[1]"Satchidanandam Brahma," NPT.U. I:6.

gunas. As all-transcendent, That is Nirguna, unaffected by the gunas. The same Supreme Being is both Saguna and Nirguna. While Bhakti-yoga is the approach to Saguna Brahman, Jnana-yoga is the approach to Nirguna Brahman. The one leads to the realization of unity with the Supreme Being; the other leads to the realization of identity with the Supreme Being. The watchword of the one is "I am His"; the watchword of the other is "I am He" or "I am That."

Sri Krishna says in the *Bhagavad-gita:*

> Through devotion, one knows Me in truth what and who I am. Then knowing Me in truth he forthwith enters into Me.
>
> (B.G. XVIII:55)

He, the Supreme Being, is the Goal of both Bhakti-yoga and Jnana-yoga. The threefold distinction of Reality is thus noted in the *Srimad Bhagavatam:*

> The knowers of Truth declare that to be the Truth — the ultimate reality, which is nondual consciousness. As all-transcendent that is called Brahman; and as immanent in the universe, that is called 'Paramatma [the all-pervading Self]' and 'Bhagavan[2] [the all-gracious God worshipped by the devotees].'
>
> (S.B. I:2.11)

As the mind is purified by the practice of Karma-yoga the aspirant develops the understanding that in this world of transitory things and beings, pleasures and possessions,

---

[2]Bhagavan is a favorite term with the devotees. Etymologically, it means the possessor of Bhaga, the six assets each in its fullness. These are glory, valor, fame, beauty, knowledge, and renunciation.

family, home, race, country, there is nothing that man can hold to as his own but God, who alone is eternal, omnipresent, all-knowing, omnipotent, and all-gracious. With the dawning of this consciousness, the aspirant becomes eligible for Bhakti-yoga.

Yet devotion to God does not grow within him simultaneously. Our thought and feeling hardly grow *pari passu* (at the same rate). The more the devotee thinks of God's love, sweetness, and grace, the greater is the possibility of the mind turning towards Him. He is the one source of all beauty, all goodness, all love, all joy.

Preparation for meditation in Bhakti-yoga means progressive development of devotion to the Supreme Being. The more the devotion grows the more the mind turns towards Him. The mark of the growth of devotion is the constant remembrance of Him by the devotee. This constant remembrance also can be counted as the very beginning of meditation. We cannot afford to forget Him whom we are devoted to, whom we love. Just as the mariner's compass turns invariably to the magnetic pole wherever the ship may go, similarly the heart of a devotee turns persistently towards God wherever he may be.

When a Karma-yogi becomes eligible for Bhakti-yoga, he may still continue his external duties as before if the situation requires it; but his actions are no longer to be counted as expressions of Karma-yoga but of Bhakti-yoga. Such Bhakti-yoga also leads to the realization of God, as explained in the following chapter.

Bhakti-yoga is also recognized by the followers of Jnana-yoga, the seekers of Nirguna Brahman. They hold that the direct approach to Nirguna Brahman is very difficult for most aspirants. After realizing Saguna Brahman through devotion, the seeker can approach Nirguna Brahman. Says Sri Krishna in the *Bhagavad-gita:*

> Greater is the difficulty of those whose minds are set on the all-transcendent Being beyond manifestation. The goal of the unmanifested One is very hard to reach for the seekers who are not free from the body-idea [who identify themselves with the body].

> (XII:5)

Broadly speaking, the path of devotion has two distinct stages. The one is the preparatory stage when the devotee has to go through rites and ceremonies —practical courses — physical, verbal, and mental; the other is the stage of spontaneous devotion. Whatever you do for the sake of the Lord with the physical body, the organ of speech, or the mind, will help you to develop devotion to Him. Of all the preparatory courses, association with the devotees of God is counted to be the most efficacious. Blessed are they who are devoted to the devotees of God.

In the *Adhyatma Ramayana*[3] Sri Ramachandra has specifically mentioned the following nine courses for the cultivation of devotion:

1. Association with My devotees.
2. Talking about Me.
3. Expounding My attributes.
4. Elucidation of My utterances and service to the preceptor with earnestness whenever possible, looking upon him as My representative.

[3] Aranya-kanda Ch.10.

5. Practice of virtue along with the observance of:
   - (a) Yama (non-violence, truthfulness, non-stealing, continence, non-covetousness).
   - (b) Niyama (cleanliness, contentment, self-control, reading of scriptures, surrendering the fruits of actions to God).
6. Daily worship of Me with steadfastness.
7. Repetition of My sacred word or formula with the pertinents, such as the use of the rosary.
8. (a) Special service to My devotees while looking upon Me in all beings.
   - (b) Dispassion to sense-objects with the serenity of mind.
9. Discussion on spiritual truths.

Sri Ramachandra further mentions in this context that any human individual whose mind turns to God is eligible for practicing these courses. He adds that whoever will persistently follow these courses, or as many as possible, will develop spontaneous devotion to God regardless of sex, caste, color, social status, and so forth. This statement has been corroborated by the lives of saints and seers throughout the ages.

From the Vedic times up to the twentieth century there have been numerous seers and sages, among women as well as men, who have been well-known for their self-dedication to spiritual idealism and for their devotional fervor.

The *Rig-Veda* mentions a number of Brahmavadinis — women seers. In the Upanishads we find the names of women saints and sages, such as Maitreyi and Gargi. In the *Ramayana* and the *Mahabharata* there are the exemplary lives of Arundhati, Sita, Savatri, Anasuya, Gandhari, Damayanti and so forth. Then in later times we find numerous ideal personalities such as Andal, Mirabai, Vishnupriya, Rani Rasmani, Holy Mother, Bhairavi Brahmani, Gopal's Mother, Ahalyabai, Rani Bhavani, Bhagavati Devi and so on.

In Buddhism, Jainism, Christianity and Islam also there have been women saints and seers. Among the women saints in Christianity we recall particularly the names of St. Catherine of Siena, Teresa of Avila, and Mother Gabrini. A well-known Moslem woman saint is Sufi Rabi'a.

Among the men devotees we would like to mention a few names of the historical period. Saint Kavir was a weaver; Ravi Das a cobbler; Sena a barber; Nama-deva of Marwar a carder of cotton; and Tukaram of Maharastra a farmer. St. Paul was a tentmaker; Jacob Boehme was a cobbler; John Bunyon was a tinsmith.

This narrative reminds us of a well-known saying of a Vaishnava savant: "The cultivation of devotion means the manifestation of the innate devotion ever existent within man."

We have said before that man is a born devotee of God; all his life he is seeking God knowingly or unknowingly.

The *Srimad Bhagavatam*[4] has mentioned the following nine practical courses:

1. Hearing about God.
2. Narration of God's glories.
3. Remembering God.

[4] VII:5.23,24.

4. Personal attendance on Divine Incarnation or the preceptor.
5. Worshipping God (including meditation on the image or the symbol with which the worship is performed).
6. Adoration of God.
7. Loving service to Divine Incarnation or the preceptor.
8. Friendly relationship with God and His devotees.
9. Self-surrender to God.

It is further said that any one of these courses followed persistently will develop ardent devotion in the heart of the seeker.

The *Svetasvatara Upanishad* concludes with an eulogy of fervent devotion:

> The truths related in this text become manifest to those great ones who develop supreme devotion to God and as much devotion to the preceptor as to God.
>
> (VI:23)

With the development of ardent devotion the devotee feels closer and closer to the Supreme Being. He contemplates more and more on His sweetness, beauty, graciousness, and love, and less and less on His splendor, might, knowledge, immensity, and so forth.

In the beginning the devotee approaches Him with a serene attitude marked with awe and veneration; the Lord of the universe is held to be far away. As he progresses in the path of devotion he feels a closer and closer relationship with Him. This develops according to the inner constitution of the devotee. The different types of relationships can be noted as follows:

1. The relationship between the Ruler and the ruled; the Preserver of the universe preserves him as well.

2. The relationship between the Master and the servant.

3. The relationship between the Parent and the child; this is two-fold:

(a) The relationship between the Father and the child.

(b) The relationship between the Mother and the child.

4. The relationship between Friend and friend. God is held to be the sole dependable friend.

5. The devotee's love becomes so intimate and deep that he approaches God with the affectionate attitude of a parent. He or she looks upon God as the divine Child. A male devotee looks upon God as the divine Child and himself as the father. A woman devotee thinks of herself as the mother and God as the divine Child. For instance, Sri Krishna's mother treated the Child Krishna with motherly affection even though she was not unaware of the child's divinity. The Madonna affectionately treated the child, Jesus, even though she was more or less conscious of His divinity.

6. The relationship wherein the devotee looks upon God as the most beloved (sweet-heart).

These relationships prevail more or less in all religions. Not a few Christian mystics held the sweet-heart attitude towards God. Through the development of any one of these

relationships the devotee can realize God. The validity of all
these relationships has been testified in the life of Sri
Ramakrishna, who saw God through each one of them.

Any relationship that appeals to a person, he should try
to hold to constantly whatever duty he may have to perform,
wherever he may have to go. By cultivating any one of these
relationships according to his inner constitution the devotee
recognizes the truth that God is all in all. He is not just the
Ruler, or just the Master, or just the Father, or just the
Friend, and so forth. He is all of these and even more,
beyond definition.

Then the devotee clasps God with all his heart, with all
his soul, with all his mind. No longer does he look upon God
as the Omnipotent, Omnipresent, Omniscient, Originator,
Ruler, Sustainer of the universe, but as his Sole Refuge, his
Sole Benefactor, his Sole Friend, his Sole Support, his Sole
Goal. There is nothing else anywhere he can hold to with
assurance.

At this stage one of the devotees thus gives expression
to his feelings:

> In this world, O Lord, in search of wealth I found Thee
> the greatest treasure. In this world, O Lord, in search of a
> friend I have found Thee the sole dependable one. In this
> world, O Lord, in search of someone to love, I have found
> Thee the most lovable one. Where else but at Thy blessed
> feet shall I seek refuge. Thou art my sole Support, my sole
> Friend, my sole Abode, my sole Goal, Thou art my All-in-
> all.

Then the devotee prays to God as stated in the *Srimad
Bhagavatam:*

May my speech be engaged in the narration of Thy attributes. May my ears be engaged in hearing about Thee. May my hands be occupied with the performance of Thy deeds. May my mind be engaged in remembering Thee. May my head be engaged in bowing down to the universe, Thy abode. May my eyes be engaged in seeing the holy men, Thy visible forms.

(S.B. X:10.38)

Whole-souled devotion is the greatest asset of human life. It is the source of incessant joy and makes man free forever.

It is said in the *Srimad Bhagavatam:*

Getting the first and foremost requisite, the human body, which is like a strong boat, so difficult to secure, yet within easy reach — with the teacher as his helmsman, and propelled by Me [God] as a favorable wind, with such means as these the man who does not strive to cross the ocean of worldly existence verily commits suicide.

(XI:20.17)

The wise man having after many births obtained this extremely rare human body, which, though frail, is yet conducive to man's supreme good, should quickly strive for liberation, before the body, which is always subject to death, chances to fall; for sense-enjoyments are available in any body.

(XI:9.29)

Earnest devotion is the golden chain by which God can be tied. If God cares for anything it is the spontaneous devotion of the human heart. Just as the devotee approaches God so also God approaches the devotee.

Says Sri Krishna in the *Bhagavad-gita:*

Persons who, giving up all other thoughts, worship Me
with their mind constantly fixed on Me, I carry to them
what they do not have and guard what they already have.
(B.G. IX:22)

With the development of fervent devotion to God the
devotee gains clear understanding of the true nature of God.
He comes to recognize the fact that God is not away from us.
He is the finest of all existences — Pure Consciousness. As
such He is the innermost Reality, the One Self of all. The
Soul of the universe is the Soul of his soul, his inmost self,
the indwelling consciousness.

Then he can meditate on God within the heart. At this
stage he needs the help of a preceptor, and God's grace also
descends on him. On these points we shall dwell in the
following chapter.

CHAPTER VIII

God-Realization through Bhakti-Yoga

In the first essay on Bhakti-yoga we have stated how from the stage of formalistic devotion an aspirant rises to the stage of natural or ardent devotion. At the same time we have noticed that he acquires the capacity to think of God as his inmost self. There are higher and higher stages of ardent devotion. Even after reaching the stage of spontaneous devotion the devotee is expected to continue such practices as association with the holy men, hearing about God, talking about God and the repetition of some name signifying Divinity, and meditation on the corresponding form as far as possible. As stated by Narada, "Devotion is attainable by continuous spiritual practice."[1]

Of all these means, association with holy men is readily efficacious. Says Sri Krishna in the *Bhagavatam:*

> He who worships Me, attaining devotion to Me through association with sages easily realizes My state taught by the sages.
>
> O, Uddhava, there is almost no other efficient way except the Bhakti-yoga due to the association with sages for I am the goal of the sages.

(XI:11.25,48)

[1] *Bhakti-sutras,* III:36.

Narada is of the opinion that devotion to God is attained primarily through the grace of a true devotee of God or through a modicum of God's grace.[2]

Devotion to God is purificatory. Nothing else can cleanse the mind as effectively. The alloy in gold cannot be extracted by any such means as washing, wiping or polishing it, but through the process of smelting it. Even so a man's subtle impressions of past karma buried in the subsoil of the mind cannot be eradicated by any physical, mental, or moral method, but by the generation of devotion within his heart.

Says Sri Krishna in the *Bhagavatam:*

> As gold smelted by fire gives up its dross and gets back its real state, so the mind by means of systematic devotion to Me winnows off subtle impressions of past karma and attains to Me.
>
> (S.B. XI:14.25)

As the mind is purified more and more devotion grows. Sri Krishna strongly recommends single-minded devotional practice.

> If even a wicked person worships Me to the exclusion of all else, he should be regarded as righteous for he is rightly resolved.
>
> Forthwith he becomes pious and attains abiding peace. O, Arjuna, you can proclaim that my devotee never perishes.
>
> (B.G. IX:30,31)

As the English word *God* is signified by different

---

[2]Bh.S. III:38.

synonyms such as Divinity, Providence, the Almighty, the Omnipresent, the Omnipotent; so there are many words in Vedantic scriptures signifying the Divine Being, such as Vishnu, Narayana, Hari, Bhagavan. They have different shades of meaning, each word fits the particular inner attitude of a devotee. The preceptor chooses the word for the devotee according to his inner constitution.

By repeating that word the devotee generates devotion suited to his or her mental make-up. With the repetition of the word Vedanta also prescribes some form corresponding to the word. Each word represents an inner idea, as does the form. The word is not just a mere sound or a combination of a few letters. The preceptor also prescribes the form corresponding to the word. While repeating the word or formula the devotee meditates on the corresponding form.

It has been stated by Narada that "devotion is the source of inexpressable joy and peace."[3] As devotion grows within, the devotee continues the practice more and more.

It has been said in the previous essay on Bhakti-yoga, that even through the performance of duties with self-surrender to God one can realize Him. "Worship [of God] is a duty for all," says Sri Krishna in the *Bhagavatam*. He continues:

> He who thus worships Me constantly and exclusively, through the performance of his duties, knowing My presence in all beings, soon attains to steadfast devotion to Me.
>
> O Uddhava, through his undying devotion he comes to Me, the great Lord of all beings, the originator and destroyer of all, their cause, the Brahman.

[3]Bh.S. IV:60.

Having his mind thus purified by the performance of his duties, and knowing My Divinity, he becomes endowed with knowledge and realization and soon attains to Me.

All this duty, consisting of specific rites, of those belonging to the castes and orders of life, if attended with devotion to Me, becomes supreme and conducive to liberation.

(S.B. XI:18.44-47)

As a devotee is drawn to God, so God is drawn to a devotee. Sri Krishna mentions in the *Bhagavad-gita* the qualifications of a true devotee which endear him to God.

He who hates no creature, and is friendly and compassionate towards all, who is free from the feelings of 'I' and 'mine,' even-minded in pain and pleasure, forbearing, ever content, steady in meditation, self-controlled, and possessed of firm conviction, with mind and intellect fixed on Me — he who is thus devoted to Me, is dear to Me.

He by whom the world is not agitated and who cannot be agitated by the world, who is freed from joy, envy, fear and anxiety — he is dear to Me.

He who is free from dependence, who is pure, prompt, unconcerned, untroubled, renouncing every worldly undertaking — he is thus devoted to Me, is dear to Me.

He who neither rejoices, nor hates, nor grieves, nor desires, renouncing good and evil, full of devotion — he is dear to Me.

He who is the same to friend and foe, and also in honour and dishonour; who is the same in heat and cold, and in pleasure and pain; who is free from attachment; to whom censure and praise are equal; who is silent, content with anything, itinerant, steady-minded, full of devotion — that one is dear to Me.

> And those who follow this perpetual way of righteousness, as described above, imbued with faith, regarding Me as the Supreme Goal, and devoted — they are exceedingly dear to Me.
>
> (B.G. XII:13-20)

As devotion grows the worshipper acquires greater and greater power of concentrating the mind on the form representing Divinity. Gradually he develops the power of concentrating the mind on the divine form within himself and on its meaning as well. For example when a fowler aims at a bird seated on a tree he sees nothing but the bird.

Sri Krishna relates to Uddhava how by meditating on God through an image a devotee can realize God as pure Consciousness dwelling within him and all-pervading.

> One should meditate on this form concentrating the mind on all the features. The person of self-control should withdraw the organs from the sense-objects with the help of the mind, and with the intellect [the determinative faculty] as guide, direct the mind to the entire form. Then he should concentrate the mind — distributed all over the form — on one part and think of the smiling countenance alone and nothing else.
>
> Drawing the mind which is concentrated on that, one should fix it on the Supreme Cause [the Lord as projecting the universe]. Then leaving this too one should rest on Me [Brahman as all-pervading Consciousness] and think of nothing whatsoever. With one's mind thus absorbed one sees God alone in one's self and sees oneself united to Him, the Self of all — the Light united to Light [state of samadhi].
>
> (S.B. XI:14.42-45)

With the continuation of devotional practices, as

devotion grows within the worshipper realizes how insignificant his efforts are in relation to the Goal he has been striving after. Naturally he prays to God for His grace at the same time.

The more the devotion grows within, the devotee surrenders himself to God more and more. With self-surrender God's grace descends upon him. As long as a person holds to his own egoistic will he is under the law of karma. But he receives divine grace when he surrenders the ego to God's supremacy.

Sri Krishna mentions in the *Bhagavad-gita* how a devotee worships God with whole-souled devotion knowing Him to be the One Self of all, how God's grace descends upon him, and how He reveals Himself unto him.

> I am the origin of all, from Me everything evolves; knowing this the wise worship Me with loving consciousness,
>
> With their minds wholly in Me, with their senses absorbed in Me, enlightening one another, and always speaking of Me, they rejoice and are delighted.
>
> To them, ever steadfast and serving Me with affection, I give that Buddhi-yoga[4] by which they come unto Me.
>
> Out of mere compassion for them, I, abiding in their hearts, destroy by the luminous lamp of knowledge the inner darkness born of ignorance.
>
> (B.G. X:8-11)

When through the grace of God the mind of the devotee apprehends the Supreme Being as the self, being identical

---

[4]Buddhi-yoga — clear grasp with the mind of My true nature as all-pervading Consciousness dwelling within as the inmost self.

with the indwelling self, then the light of the Supreme Being shines in the mental mode, which serves as the shining lamp that removes the underlying ajnana (the darkness of inapprehension that hides the Supreme Being). When this ajnana is removed, then the Supreme Being becomes self-revealed in samadhi.[5]

He who realizes God within also sees God in all beings. Just as God is worshipped in an image even so he can be worshipped in a living being as the indwelling self. In his last message Sri Krishna speaks highly of this form of worship. In the *Bhagavad-gita* He has thus praised this spiritual outlook:

> With the heart concentrated by Yoga, with the eye of evenness for all things, he beholds the Self in all beings and all beings in the Self.
>
> He who sees Me in all things, and sees all things in Me, he never becomes separated from Me, nor do I become separated from him.
>
> He who being established in unity, worships Me, who am dwelling in all beings, whatever his mode of life, that Yogi abides in Me.
>
> He who judges of pleasure or pain everywhere, by the same standard as he applies to himself, that Yogi, O Arjuna, is regarded as the highest.
>
> (B.G. VI:29-32)

Says Sri Krishna to Uddhava:

> With a pure mind one should observe in all beings as well as in oneself only Me, the Atman, who am both within and without, and all-pervasive like space.

[5]For further explanation see Madhusudana Saraswati's commentary.

O great soul, he who, taking his stand on pure knowledge, thus regards and honors all beings as myself, who has the same attitude towards a low born one as to a Brahmana, towards a thief as to a supporter of the Brahmanas, towards a spark of fire as to the sun, and towards a ruffian as to a kind man; he is considered a sage.

Ideas of rivalry, jealousy, pity and egoism quickly depart from a man who always thinks of Me in all men.

One should worship thus in thought, word, and deed till one comes to look upon all beings as Myself.

To such a man everything is Brahman [the Supreme Being] owing to the knowledge that comes of seeing the Atman in all. Seeing Brahman everywhere, he becomes free from doubts and all attachment. This looking upon all beings as Myself in thought, word, and deed is, to My mind, the best of all methods of worship.

Herein lies the wisdom of the wise and the acumen of the intelligent, that in this very life they attain Me, the Real and Immortal, by means of that which is unreal and mortal.

(S.B. XI:29.12-15,17-19,22)

The culmination of devotion is in seeing and worshipping God in all living beings. Here devotion is united with supreme spiritual vision. The highest devotion is inseparable from the highest knowledge. It is said in the *Bhagavatam:*

He who sees the divine Self in all beings and all beings in the divine Self is the best devotee of God. He who bears love to God, friendship to His devotees, kindness to the ignorant, indifference to his foes, is of the second best type, and he who faithfully worships God only in the image, and not His devotees or others, is a novice.
(S.B. XI:2.45-47)

That this mode of seeing and worshipping God in all

beings is natural with the seers and the lovers of God who attain illumination, has been affirmed by the Upanishads and by later Vedantic literature.

> The wise man beholds all beings in the Self, and the Self in all beings; for that reason he does not dislike anyone.
> (I.U. 6)

> Thou art the woman, Thou art the man, Thou art the youth and the maiden too. Thou art the old man who totters along, leaning on the staff. Thou art born with faces turned in all directions.
> (Sv.U. IV:3)

Rare individuals, highly advanced in spiritual life, have also carried this idea into actual practice. But so far the seekers of God in general have not adopted this way of worship as a spiritual discipline. Such a course has been recommended for the first time by Sri Ramakrishna in the present age. "No, not kindness to living beings," he urges, "but service to God dwelling in them."[6]

"If God can be worshipped through a clay image, then why not through a man?" he used to say.[7] In his view, it is God who exists in all forms, though His manifestations differ.

It was the genius of Swami Vivekananda to find new light in this precept of the Master and seek its practical application in modern life for the amelioration of man's condition in every sphere. He exhorts the worshippers of God to follow this method:

[6]See *Sri Ramakrishna, the Great Master,* by Swami Saradananda, p. 821. Ramakrishna Math, Madras, India: 1952.

[7]*Gospel,* p.407.

"Look upon every man, woman, and every one as God. You cannot help anyone; you can only serve; serve the children of the Lord, serve the Lord Himself, if you have the privilege. If the Lord grants that you can help any one of His children, blessed you are; do not think too much of yourselves. Blessed you are that that privilege was given to you, when others had it not. Do it only as worship."[8]

"You may invent an image through which to worship God, but a better image already exists, the living man. You may build a temple in which to worship God, and that may be good, but a better one, a much higher one, already exists; the human body."[9]

In Swami Vivekananda's view all social work and the teaching of religion as well should be carried on in the spirit of worshipping God in man. For this purpose he established the Ramakrishna Math and Mission — a religious and philanthropic institution that has developed into a world-wide organization — the monastic and lay members of which are urged to render service to the ignorant, the needy, the distressed, and the diseased, as the veritable worship of God dwelling in them.

[8]"Vedanta in Its Application to Indian Life," C.W., Vol. III, p. 246.
[9]"Practical Vedanta," pt.2. C.W., Vol. II, p.311.

CHAPTER IX

The Process of Meditation According to Patanjali's Raja-Yoga; Distinctiveness of the Vedantic Method

According to the dualistic Samkhya system of Kapila, which Patanjali has adopted with some differences in delineating the method of Yoga, the self-intelligent purusha and the non-intelligent prakriti are the two distinct fundamental principles. Purusha is of the nature of consciousness, pure and simple, and is changeless; whereas prakriti, the origin of all psychical and physical elements, is altogether devoid of consciousness and subject to change in proximity to purusha, like iron moving near a magnet. While prakriti is one, purushas are many.

In the Samkhya-Yoga view, all objects, psychical and physical, have evolved from prakriti, primordial nature — a state of equilibrium of the three gunas. Evolution starts with the disturbance of this balance. The successive transformations of prakriti are mahat (the pure mind-stuff); egoism; the internal organ or the mind; the five organs of perception; the five organs of action; the five subtle elements; and the five gross elements; all of which have successively evolved from prakriti. Thus, there are twenty-four categories of objects, including prakriti. Together with purusha, there are altogether twenty-five principles according to Kapila, the founder of Samkhya system.[1]

The first and finest product of prakriti — mahat, is also called *buddhi-sattva*, the pure mind-stuff in which the principle of sattva is predominant. It is transparent and pervasive by nature. Being reflected in mahat or buddhi-sattva, purusha is identified with it. Because of this association they seemingly partake of each other's characteristics, somewhat like the sun and the mirror in which it is reflected.

Buddhi-sattva, which is intrinsically non-intelligent, appears to be intelligent or conscious; and purusha, which is changeless consciousness, ever pure, free, and luminous, appears to undergo such changing states as knowledge and ignorance, pain and pleasure, virtue and vice, bondage and freedom, which are the modes of buddhi-sattva.

Due to its association with buddhi-sattva, purusha turns out to be *the seer* or the experiencer, and prakriti to be *the seen* or the experienced. All transformation of prakriti is for the experience and the liberation of *the seer*.[2]

Thus begins the erroneous identification of the self with the not-self.[3] This is the primary cause of the jiva's miseries, according to both Samkhya-yoga and Vedanta. "The union of the seer and the seen is the cause of suffering to be prevented," says Patanjali. "Ignorance is its root."[4] Like a pure crystal appearing red in proximity to a red flower, *the*

---

[1] See *Samkhya-darsanam*, Aphorism I:61, and Vijnana Bhikhsnu's commentary.

[2] Y.A. II:21.

[3] *Samkhya-karika* 20,21.

[4] Y.A. II:17,24.

seer appears to be bound to prakriti and its modifications in association with them.[5] Its closest association is, of course, with buddhi-sattva.

The freedom of the self consequently means its complete withdrawal and aloofness from prakriti and its transformations, gross and subtle. This is achieved through sharp discrimination of the self from the not-self, particularly from buddhi-sattva. Keen introspection and intense meditation, with preparatory steps, are essential requisites for such an end.

One important point of difference between Samkhya and Yoga is this: Kapila, the founder of the Samkhya system, does not recognize an eternal God (Isvara); while Patanjali recognizes Isvara as the First Teacher. "Existence of God cannot be established," says Kapila.[6] According to Patanjali, "He (Isvara) is the teacher of even the ancient teachers being unlimited by time."[7]

It is to be noted that while Samkhya-Yoga aims at the removal of all sufferings of the self, *the seer*,[8] Vedanta aims in reinstating the self in its pristine blissfulness as is evident from the following versions:

> There is one Supreme Ruler, the inmost Self of all beings, who makes His one form manifold. Eternal happiness belongs to the wise, who perceive Him within themselves — not to others.
>
> (Ka.U. II:2.12)

[5]Sd. I:19; II:35.
[6]Sd. I:92.
[7]Y.A. I:26.
[8]Sk. 3.

Eternal happiness belongs to the wise who realize within themselves the presence of Him, the One Ruler, who diversifies the one seed of inert multiplicity. To none else belongs eternal happiness.

(Sv.U. VI:12)

He who realizes the bliss of Brahman has nothing to fear.

(Tai.U. II:4.1)

The *Yoga Aphorisms of Patanjali*[9] is the first comprehensive treatment of the system of Raja-yoga. It consists of four sections (called Padas, lit. quarters). The first section dwells mainly on samadhi (realization of the self as distinct from prakriti as its knower); the second section on sadhana, the practical courses of yoga; the third section on bibhuti, supernatural powers attainable by yoga practice; the fourth on kaivalya, aloofness of the self from prakriti, as its knower.

In the beginning of the book Patanjali has defined yoga. "Yoga is subduing the modifications of the mind stuff." This being achieved the knower (the self) abides in its true nature, as distinct from prakriti, which is known. Yoga is attained by practice and dispassion. The practice becomes well-grounded by long-continued effort with zeal without break.

We are particularly concerned with the second chapter where Patanjali delineates the eight steps of Raja-yoga, culminating in samadhi. (See Aphorism II:29) These are:

[9]With the commentary of Vyasa and the explanatory note of Vachaspati Misra and others. Ananda Ashrama Sanskrit series, No.47. Poona:1932.

1. **Yama** — non-violence, truthfulness, non-stealing, continence, non-covetousness.

Non-violence: not hurting anyone by thought, word or deed.

Continence: the source of strength.

Non-covetousness: not to possess anything more than what is essential.

2. **Niyama** — cleanliness, contentment, austerity, study, worship of God.

Cleanliness: purification of the body and the mind. When the mind is purified it becomes calm.

As stated by Patanjali, calmness of the mind can be achieved by amity to those who are happy, compassion for those who are suffering, esteem for the virtuous, and disregard to those who are dishonest.[10]

"Contentment is the source of greatest happiness," says Patanjali.[11]

Austerity, study, and worship of God (Isvara) are distinguished by Patanjali as the courses of action.[12] The rest may be counted as rules of conduct.

Austerity: the practice of controlling the body, of controlling the organ of speech (particularly) and of controlling the mind. The control of the organ of speech leads to the control of the other organs.

Study of the scriptures for spiritual development and the repetition of the sacred word or formula — japa.

Worship of God: surrendering the fruits of action to God.

[10] Y.A. I:33.
[11] Y.A. II:42.
[12] Y.A. II:1.

We have already mentioned that Patanjali recognizes Isvara as the teacher of teachers, the First Teacher. The verbal symbol of Isvara is "OM," the repetition of which, with the apprehension of its meaning, is very efficacious.

One can attain samadhi through the worship of God as well.[13]

3. *Asana* — the sitting posture that makes the body steady and comfortable.

The following postures are generally regarded as conducive to steadiness of the body and the mind: Padmasana, Siddhasana, Svastikasana, Sukhasana and Samasana. Through the practice of asana one increases the power of endurance of heat and cold.

4. *Pranayama* — practice of regular inhalation, exhalation and retention of breath.

It is conducive to the calmness of the body and the mind. It soothes the nerves. (It is proper to learn the practice from an adept.)

5. *Pratyahara* — gathering up the sense-organs from the external objects and turning them inward to the object of meditation.

Instead of letting the mind turn toward the organs, the organs should be turned toward the mind. This leads to the control of the organs.

6. *Dharana* — the first step toward meditation; fixing the mind to the object of concentration, which may be external or internal.

7. *Dhyana (meditation)* — through the practice of Dharana, one should be able to hold the mind for 144

[13]Y.A. II:45.

seconds on the object of meditation at the first stage.

Three factors are there in meditation — the meditator, the object of meditation and the act of meditation. In samadhi this tripartite distinction does not prevail.

8. *Samadhi* — Patanjali thus distinguishes between meditation and samadhi:

> Meditation is the uninterrupted concentration of thought on its object. This itself turns into samadhi when the object alone shines and the thought of meditation (and of the meditator) is lost as it were.
>
> (Y.A. III:2,3)

Dharana is intervened by contrary thoughts; when uninterrupted by contrary thoughts Dharana turns into Dhyana. In Dhyana there are three factors — the object of meditation, the act of meditation and the meditator. In samadhi only the object of meditation shines. This continued for some time is samprajnata samadhi. When even the object of meditation drops, then it turns into asamprajnata samadhi.[14]

In the third chapter Patanjali has dwelt on miraculous powers, which can be developed by various methods of meditation. He also mentions that though these may serve some purpose in the empirical life, they are obstacles to samadhi (Aphorism III:37). In order to gain Kaivalya (Liberation) one must disregard them (Aphorism III:50).

Vedanta also holds the view that occult powers (vibhuti) can be developed by different methods of meditation but they do not have spiritual value. This will be

[14]Further explained on page 205.

evident from the following parable recorded in *The Gospel of Sri Ramakrishna*. In the words of Sri Ramakrishna:

"It is very troublesome to possess occult powers. Nangta (Tota Puri) taught me this by a story. A man who had acquired occult powers was sitting on the seashore when a storm arose. It caused him great discomfort; so he said, 'Let the storm stop.' His words could not remain unfulfilled. At that moment a ship was going full sail before the wind. When the storm ceased abruptly the ship capsized and sank. The passengers perished and the sin of causing their death fell to the man. And because of that sin he lost his occult powers and went to hell.

"Once upon a time a sadhu acquired great occult powers. He was vain about them. But he was a good man and had some austerities to his credit. One day the Lord, disguised as a holy man, came to him and said, 'Revered sir, I have heard that you have great occult powers.' The sadhu received the Lord cordially and offered him a seat. Just then an elephant passed by. The Lord, in the disguise of the holy man, said to the sadhu, 'Revered sir, can you kill this elephant if you like?' The sadhu said, 'Yes, it is possible.'

"So saying, he took a pinch of dust, muttered some mantras over it, and threw it at the elephant. The beast struggled awhile in pain and then dropped dead. The Lord said: 'What power you have! You have killed the elephant!' The sadhu laughed. Again the Lord spoke: 'Now can you revive the elephant?' 'That too is possible,' replied the sadhu. He threw another pinch of charmed dust at the beast. The elephant writhed about a little and came back to life.

Then the Lord said: 'Wonderful is your power. But may

I ask you one thing? You have killed the elephant and you have revived it. But what has that done for you? Do you feel uplifted by it? Has it enabled you to realize God?' Saying this the Lord vanished."[15]

Truly speaking, these eight steps of Raja-yoga form the common basis of Bhakti-yoga, and Jnana-yoga as well; Vedanta recognizes the practical courses of Patanjali but not his philosophical basis, which is dualistic. As mentioned in the *Srimad Bhagavatam*, there are three main yogas — Karma-yoga, Bhakti-yoga and Jnana-yoga. Sri Krishna says to Uddhava, "I have spoken of three yogas with the object of conferring supreme good on human beings."[16]

We find references to the practical courses of yoga in the *Svetasvatara Upanishad* and later scriptures:

> Placing the body in a straight posture, holding the chest, throat and head erect, and drawing the senses and the mind into the heart [the location of the self] the aspirant should cross over all the fearful currents by means of the raft of Brahman [repetition of the verbal symbols of Brahman].

> Controlling the senses with an effort, and regulating the movements in the body, one should breathe out through the nostrils when the vital forces become gentle. Then the aspirant, without being in the least distracted, should keep his hold on the mind as on the reins attached to restive horses.

> One should practice concentration, resorting to caves and such other agreeable places helpful to its practice — where the ground is free from pebbles, fire, sand, wind, and sound of water courses, where the scenery is pleasing to the eyes.

[15]*Gospel*, p. 547.
[16]S.B. XI:20.3.

It is said that the first marks of progress in yoga practice are lightness of body, good health, thirstlessness of mind, clearness of complexion, sweetness of voice, aroma of the body, and scantiness of excretions.

(Sv.U. II:8-10,13)

In the Brahma Sutras, we also find the following references to yoga practice:

One has to practice Upasana (contemplation on God) sitting, because [in that way alone] it is possible.

And on account of meditation [implying that].

Wherever concentration of mind [is attained], there [it is to be practiced], there being no specification [as to place].

(B.S. IV:1.7,8,11)

In the *Bhagavad-gita* Sri Krishna thus relates yoga practice:

The Yogi should constantly practice concentration of the mind, retiring into solitude all by himself, with the mind and body subdued, and free from hankering and possession.

Having in a clean spot established his seat, firm, neither too high nor too low, made of Kusha-grass, deerskin and cloth arranged consecutively.

There, seated on that seat, making the mind one-pointed and subduing the wanderings of the senses and the mind, he should practice Yoga for self-purification.

Let him firmly hold his body, head and neck erect and still, gazing at the tip of his nose, and not looking around.

With the intellect [buddhi]serene and fearless, firm in the vow of celibacy, with the mind composed, and ever

contemplating on Me, let him sit [in Yoga] having Me as
his supreme goal.

Thus always keeping the intellect [buddhi] steadfast,
the Yogi of subdued mind attains the peace residing in Me
— the peace which culminates in Nirvana (Moksha).

(B.G. VI:10-15)

Both Yoga and Vedanta stress the practice of
meditation as the means of Self-realization. In fact, Vedanta
accepts the eightfold practical course of Yoga in spite of
differences in their philosophical views. But their methods
of meditation are not the same. The whole method of Yoga
is based on the Samkhya system of Kapila, which Patanjali
has adopted with a few divergences. In the realization of the
Self, Samkhya-Yoga has followed primarily the method of
the withdrawal of the self from the not-self, particularly
from the buddhi-sattva (the pure mind-stuff), with which it
has the closest relation.

In deep meditation on the *grahita*, the experiencer,
which is the self identified with buddhi-sattva, the yogi
discerns the two, and realizes the self as distinct from the
other. A clear and steady perception of the self as other than
buddhi-sattva is called *viveka-khyati* (lit., discriminating
knowledge). It counteracts *avidya* (wrong knowledge), the
primal cause of the identification of the self with the not-self.
As stated by Patanjali:

The cause of this [the identification of the self with
buddhi-sattva] is avidya [wrong knowledge].

When avidya has been eradicated, the identification
ceases. Then bondage drops, as the experiencer becomes
aloof [that is, reinstated in its innate freedom].

The way to eradicate avidya and sever bondage is the constant apprehension of the self as other than buddhi-sattva.

At the seventh stage of this [discriminating] knowledge the yogi reaches its highest level.

(Y.A. II:24-27)

Even then the Self is not realized. Being firmly established in samprajnata samadhi, the yogi develops the power to enter into asamprajnata samadhi, which is the complete withdrawal of the self from buddhi-sattva. By supreme detachment he foregoes even the knowledge that the self is altogether different from buddhi-sattva. For he realizes that this discriminating knowledge, howsoever high it may be, is a mode of buddhi-sattva to which the self has no relation at all. So he becomes completely withdrawn from buddhi-sattva, and the knowledge that is manifest in it. Then buddhi-sattva being absolutely free from all modes and contentless, becomes perfectly calm and restored to its pristine purity. This is the state of asamprajnata samadhi, in which there is no cognition of any kind whatsoever. This is preparatory to Liberation (Kaivalya).[17]

Vedanta also recommends the discrimination of the self from the not-self. But after being aware of the true nature of the self through discrimination, the aspirant has to fix the mind on the Self and the Self alone. Nothing else should be contemplated. So it is said:

The Self alone is to be meditated upon, for all these [the limiting adjuncts] are unified in It [having no separate existence].

[17]Y.A. I:51; IV:34.

> Of all these, this Self alone should be realized, for one knows all these through It, just as one may track [an animal] through its footprints.
>
> (Br.U. I:4.7)

For the realization of Brahman, Saguna or Nirguna, the thoughts must be concentrated thereon. Says Sri Krishna: "Fix thy mind on Me, be devoted to Me, sacrifice unto Me. Thus, having thy mind steadfast in Me, with Me as thy Supreme Goal, thou shalt reach Me [the Self of all beings]."[18] Again, "Fix thy mind exclusively in Me, fasten thy intellect on Me; Thou shalt no doubt live in Me hereafter."[19]

[18] B.G. IX:34.
[19] B.G. XII:8.

CHAPTER X

Preparation for Meditation in Jnana-Yoga

Jnana-yoga, the path of knowledge, is the way to the realization of the identity of the adherent's inmost self[1] with Nirguna Brahman. Finally the self merges in the Ultimate Reality, the One without a second, beyond thought, beyond word. By implication this is said to be Nondual Brahman; pure Being, Consciousness, Bliss.

As declared by the Upanishads:

> Brahman is Truth, Consciousness, Infinite.
> (Tai.U. II:1.3)
>
> Brahman is Consciousness, Bliss.
> (Br.U. III:9.28.7)
>
> Supreme Brahman is Being-Consciousness-Bliss.
> (NPT.U. I:6)

The manifold we experience has no Ultimate Reality. The fundamental One is the substratum of the apparent manifold, the playground of diversities. The apparent multiplicity does not affect the underlying Reality, just as mirage water does not moisten the sandy bed of the desert. Nondual Brahman is all-in-all. It interpenetrates each and every finite form of living and non-living. Though immanent

[1]Also called "Sakshi-chaitanya (witness-self)," and "Kutastha-chaitanya (rock-steady self)."

in the universe it is all-transcendent. As such it is called Nirguna Brahman, unaffected by diversities.

Verily, "All this is Brahman," declares the *Chhandogya Upanishad* (III:14.1). So says the *Mundaka Upanishad:*

> The immortal Brahman alone is before, that Brahman is behind, that Brahman is to the right and to the left. Brahman alone pervades everything above and below; this universe is that Supreme Brahman alone.
>
> (Mu.U. II:2.12)

It is further said in the same *Upanishad* with regard to Brahman:

> That is all-pervasive and self-effulgent; and Its nature is inconceivable. It is subtler than the subtle. It shines diversely. It is further away than the far-off, and It is near at hand in this body. By the seers It is [perceived as] seated in this very body, in the cavity of the heart.[2]
>
> This is not comprehended through the eye nor through the other senses; nor expressed by the organ of speech. Nor is It attainable through austerity or karma. When one becomes purified in mind through the clarity of understanding, then can one see that indivisible Self through meditation.
>
> (III:1.7,8)

Nondual Brahman underlying the manifold is the One Self of the multiform universe and of every individual thing and being. The existence of each and everything is due to that Basic Reality, Being — Consciousness — Bliss. It penetrates each and every finite form, living and non-living.

---

[2] See Appendix II, "The Location of the Soul in the Body."

It is specially manifest in the sentient. Each and every individual is essentially That. This is because the Supreme Being — pure Being, Consciousness, Bliss — is the indwelling Self of every human being. This is why the Self is the dearest of all. Whatever is loved is for the sake of the Self.

The supreme purpose of human life is to realize the identity of the indwelling Self with Nirguna Brahman, the all-transcendent Supreme Being. Finally the individual self is known to be the Self of all. Man's inmost self is the central principle of consciousness in the psychophysical constitution, which cognizes not only the external objects but also the conditions and functions of the body, the organs, and the mind. It is beyond the ego. This is the first object of man's love and is identical with the universal Self.

We recall in this context the anecdote of Yajnavalkya and Maitreyi in the *Brihadaranyaka Upanishad*:[3]

> Yajnavalkya had two wives: Maitreyi and Katyayani. Of these, Maitreyi was conversant with the knowledge of Brahman, while Katyayani had an essentially feminine outlook. One day Yajnavalkya, when he decided to embrace monastic life, said:
>
> "Maitreyi, my dear, I am going to renounce this life (to become a monk). Let me make a final settlement between you and Katyayani."
>
> Maitreyi said: "Venerable Sir, if indeed the whole earth full of wealth belonged to me, would I be immortal through that or not?" "No," replied Yajnavalkya. "Your life would be just like that of people who have plenty. Of immortality, however, there is no prospect through wealth."

[3] IV:5.1-6,15.

Then Maitreyi said: "What should I do with that which would not make me immortal? Tell me, venerable Sir, of that alone which you know [to be the only means of attaining immortality]."

Yajnavalkya replied: "My dear, you have been my beloved [even before], and [now] you have resolved [to know] what is after my heart. If you wish, my dear, I shall explain it to you. As I explain it, meditate [on what I say]."

"Verily, not for the sake of the husband, my dear, is the husband loved, but he is loved for the sake of the self [which, in its true nature, is one with the Supreme Self].

"Verily, not for the sake of the wife, my dear, is the wife loved, but she is loved for the sake of the self.

"Verily, not for the sake of the sons, my dear, are the sons loved, but they are loved for the sake of the self.

"Verily, not for the sake of wealth, my dear, is wealth loved, but it is loved for the sake of the self.

"Verily, not for the sake of the animals, my dear, are the animals loved, but they are loved for the sake of the self.

"Verily, not for the sake of the brahmin, my dear, is the brahmin loved, but he is loved for the sake of the self.

"Verily, not for the sake of the kshatriya, my dear, is the kshatriya loved, but he is loved for the sake of the self.

"Verily, not for the sake of the all, my dear, is the all loved, but it is loved for the sake of the self.

"Verily, my dear Maitreyi, it is the Self that should be realized — should be heard of, reflected on, and meditated upon. By the realization of the Self, my dear, through hearing, reflection, and meditation, all this is known.

"Thus you have the instruction given to you. This much, indeed, is [the means to] Immortality."

After giving the instruction Yajnavalkya left home.

As a result of the practice of Karma-yoga subsidiary to Jnana-yoga (which we have discussed in a previous chapter), the aspirant develops the following four requisites for the attainment of Self-knowledge (Vc. 19):

1. The discrimination of the Real and the unreal: that is Real which never goes out of existence; what is unreal has no existence. Also the consequent conviction that Brahman is real, the manifold is unreal. It only appears to exist.[4]

2. Aversion to the enjoyment of the fruits of actions here and hereafter.

3. Six assets: (1) Serenity of the mind; (2) Self-control; (3) Fortitude; (4) Dispassion; (5) Faith in the words of the scriptures and the preceptor; (6) Having the Goal constantly in mind.

4. Hankering after Liberation.

In the *Bhagavad-gita* Sri Krishna mentions the following subsidiary qualifications as conducive to Self-knowledge, which are the keys to Liberation or Immortality.

> Humility, unpretentiousness, non-injury, forbearance, uprightness, service to the teacher, purity, steadiness, self-control;
>
> The dispassion for sense-objects, and also absence of egoism; reflection on the evils of birth, death, old age, sickness and pain;
>
> Non-attachment, non-identification of the self with son, wife, home, and the rest, and constant even-mindedness in the occurrence of the desirable and the undesirable;
>
> Unswerving devotion to Me by the Yoga of non-separation, resort to sequestered place, distaste for association with men;

[4]See Appendix III, "The Sum and Substance of Advaita Vedanta."

> Constant application to spiritual knowledge, un-
> derstanding of the end of true knowledge — this is
> declared to be conducive to Self-knowledge, and what is
> contrary to it causes ignorance.
>
> (B.G. XIII:7-11)

A competent seeker of Self-knowledge has to go
invariably to a proficient teacher. The necessity of
approaching an adept teacher on the part of a qualified
spiritual aspirant has been very much emphasized in the
Vedantic literature.

It is said in the *Mundaka Upanishad:*

> Thoroughly investigating into the realms attainable by
> work, the seeker of Self-knowledge should be dis-
> passionate. The eternal cannot be the product of work. In
> order to realize the Truth he should positively approach
> with faggots in hand [a mark of humility and readiness to
> serve] the teacher who is well versed in the Vedas and
> established in the knowledge of Brahman.
>
> (Mu.U. I:2.12)

(Shankaracharya remarks in this context that even
though possessed of knowledge of the scriptures the pupil
should not independently seek the direct knowledge of
Brahman.)

Sri Krishna says in the *Bhagavad-gita:*

> Know that [the Truth], by prostrating thyself, by
> queries, and by service; the wise, who have realized the
> Truth, will instruct thee in that knowledge.
>
> (B.G. IV:34)

Says Shankaracharya in his *Viveka-chudamani:*

The inquirer about the truth of the Atman who is possessed of the above-mentioned four means of attainment [p.211] should approach a wise preceptor, who is capable of deliverance;

Who is versed in the Vedas, taintless, unsmitten by desire and a knower of Brahman par excellence, who is settled in Brahman, is calm like fire that has consumed its fuel, who is a boundless reservoir of mercy by nature and a benefactor of all good people who prostrate themselves before him.

(Vc. 32,33)

Even a scholar well versed in the Vedic texts often fails to grasp the central truths declared by them. For the profitable study of the Vedas the pupil has not only to get acquainted with the core of the Vedic teachings, but also to be convinced of their rationality. Above all, he has to adopt practical methods to realize the spiritual truths. For all these purposes the guidance of an efficient spiritual teacher is indispensable. The teacher points out the central teachings, convinces the pupil of their reasonableness by arguments, and also instructs the pupil on the practical courses for realizing the truth. For this three-fold reason particularly, the necessity for the guidance of an adept has been emphasized in Vedanta.

It is said in the *Katha Upanishad:*

Many there are who do not have the chance to hear of Atman. Though hearing of Atman, many cannot comprehend That. Wonderful is the expounder and rare is the hearer; rare indeed is the experiencer of Atman, being taught by an able preceptor.

Atman when taught by an incompetent person, is not easily comprehended, because It is diversely regarded by disputants. But when It is taught by him who has realized his identity with Atman, there can remain no more doubt about It. Atman is subtler than the subtlest and not to be known through argumentation.

(Ka.U. I:2.7,8)

The identity of the individual self and the Supreme Self is the quintessence of the Vedic knowledge. In each of the four Vedas there is a terse sentence delivering this knowledge. This is called *Mahavakya,* lit. the Great Saying. It points to the identity of the individual self with Nirguna Brahman, and not with the Ultimate Reality beyond thought, beyond word.

In the *Aitareya Upanishad* of the *Rig-Veda* the Mahavakya is "Consciousness is Brahman." The meaning is that the indwelling consciousness in an individual is identical with Brahman, the Supreme Being.[5]

In the *Brihadaranyaka Upanishad* of the *Yajur-Veda,* the Great Saying is "I am Brahman." (One's inmost self is (Nirguna) Brahman.)[6]

In the *Chhandogya Upanishad* of the *Sama-Veda,* the Great Saying is "That Thou Art."[7] The sage Uddalaka imparted the lesson to his son, Svetaketu, that everything in the universe is permeated by One Self, All-pervading Consciousness. So every individual is essentially That.

In the *Mandukya Upanishad* of the *Atharva-Veda* the Great Saying is "This self is Brahman." One's innermost self is essentially Nondual Consciousness.[8]

[5]Ai.U. III:1.3.
[6]Br.U. I:4.10.
[7]Ch.U. VI:8.7.
[8]Ma.U. II.

"This supreme Vedic teaching (Mahavakya) imparts a twofold knowledge attainable by no other means: on the one hand, by affirming atman as Brahman, it removes man's deep-rooted misconception regarding himself, namely, that he is bound, finite, imperfect, and mortal; and points to his true self as self-existent, self-shining, ever-pure and ever-free. On the other hand, by proclaiming Brahman as atman it removes man's equally indomitable misconception regarding the Supreme Being, namely, that He is remote, unattainable, hidden, if not non-existent, and reveals Him as the innermost Self, ever-manifest, immediate and direct. Thus, what is conceived as the farthest is revealed as nearer than the nearest, what appears to be unattainable as already attained, what is ever hidden as self-manifest."[9]

Each of these terse sentences declares the identity of the individual consciousness and the universal or all-pervading consciousness, and points to the sole reality of Nondual Consciousness that Brahman is. Hence, this great teaching (Mahavakya) is said to be *akhandartha-bodhaka* (indicative of the Undivided Absolute Being free from all distinctions).

We recall in this context Shankaracharya's hymn *Nirvana-Satkam* (Six stanzas on Nirvana). This is also called *Atma-Satkam* (Six stanzas on the Self).

Om, I am neither mind, nor intellect, nor ego, nor chitta;[10]

[9]The author's *Methods of Knowledge (According to Advaita Vedanta)*, pp.200-201. George Allen & Unwin Ltd., London:1965. Advaita Ashrama, Mayavati, India: 1974.

[10]These are responsible for four different functions of the cognitive aspect of the mind (antahkarana): 1) Deliberation, 2) Determination, 3) I-ness, and 4) Recollection.

Neither ears nor tongue nor the senses of smell and sight;
Nor am I ether, earth, fire, water, or air:
I am Pure Consciousness and Bliss: I am Shiva! I am Shiva!

I am neither the prana nor the five vital breaths;
Neither the seven elements of the body nor its five sheaths;
Nor hands nor feet nor tongue, nor the organs of sex and
   elimination:
 I am Pure Consciousness and Bliss: I am Shiva! I am Shiva!

Neither loathing nor liking have I, neither greed nor delusion;
No sense have I of ego or pride, neither dharma nor moksha;
Neither desire of the mind nor object for its desiring:
I am Pure Consciousness and Bliss: I am Shiva! I am Shiva!

Neither virtue nor vice am I, neither pleasure nor pain;
Nor the mantra, the sacred place, the Vedas, the sacrifice;
Neither the act of eating, the eater, nor the food:
I am Pure Consciousness and Bliss: I am Shiva! I am Shiva!

Death or fear I have none, nor any distinction of caste;
Neither father nor mother nor even a birth have I;
Neither friend nor comrade, neither disciple nor guru:
I am Pure Consciousness and Bliss: I am Shiva! I am Shiva!

I have no form or fancy, the All-pervading am I;
Everywhere I exist, yet I am beyond the senses;
Neither salvation nor bondage have I, nor anything
   that may be known:
I am Pure Consciousness and Bliss: I am Shiva! I am Shiva!

For the practice of meditation on the atman as identical
with Brahman, it is absolutely necessary for the seeker of
Truth to have the previous knowledge of atman and of
Brahman from a reliable source, that is to say, from the
scriptures and the words of the preceptor. Next he should
form a clear idea of the nature of both (atman and Brahman)
by contemplation. Then he has to be convinced of the Truth
of their identity through reasoning. When he forms a
definite idea in his mind of Nirguna Brahman, with firm

conviction, then he can meditate on the Self as Brahman.

The practice of meditation is an attempt to make the mental mode conform with Reality. The more the mental mode conforms with Reality the more the light of Reality shines in the mental mode. Realization comes with the full conformity of the mental mode with Reality, as the light of Reality shining in the mental mode removes the underlying primal ajnana. The threefold methods by which this is achieved are known as: 1) Hearing (sravana), 2) Contemplation (manana), and 3) Persistent practice of meditation (nididhyasana).

So it is said in the *Mundaka Upanishad:*

> That Brahman is vast, self-luminous, inconceivable, subtler than the subtle. That shines forth. That is far beyond what is far, and yet here very near at hand. That is seen here, dwelling in the cave of the heart of conscious beings. Brahman is not grasped by the eye, nor by the organ of speech, nor by other organs or senses, nor by penance nor righteous deed. Being pure-minded through the purity of understanding, as a person practices meditation, thereby he beholds Him, who is whole and without component parts.
>
> (Mu.U. III:1.7,8)

CHAPTER XI

Realization of Nondual Brahman, the Culmination of Jnana-Yoga

From time immemorial the Supreme Vedic knowledge regarding the indwelling self (Sakshichaitanya) and Brahman and their identity has been transmitted to the modern age in an unbroken line of preceptors and disciples. After the temporary arrest of its progress during the prevalence of Buddhism, it was Sri Shankaracharya who revived the Vedic religion and reestablished it on an unshaken foundation in the beginning of the eighth century A.D. He came of a well-known orthodox Brahmin family of Kalady in Kerala State in the Province of Malabar in Southwest India. He was thoroughly steeped in the Vedic lore. He lived a short life of 32 years, approximately 686-718 A.D. Nevertheless his achievements were prodigious.

Even as a boy Shankara was calm and contemplative. His intellect and memory were amazing. By the time he was seven years old he had finished the whole course of the Vedic studies under a scholarly tutor, who was astounded by the pupil's merit. The boy's profound scholarship and wisdom won the admiration of one and all; his fame extended far and wide. But learning and fame, wealth and position, meant little to young Shankara, whose mind yearned for the experience of the Supreme Truth, the sole reality of Brahman. He decided to leave home and approach the great teacher Govindapada, an illustrious knower of Brahman, for instruction and initiation into the monastic life (sannyasa).

At Onkarnath on the river Narmada, Shankara lived under the guidance of his guru about three years and realized Nondual Brahman in nirvikalpa samadhi. As a result of this experience his heart was filled with spontaneous love for one and all, urging him to enlighten their minds and guide them on the way to supreme peace and blessedness. The following sloka in his *Viveka-chudamani* is reminiscent of Shankara himself.

> There are great souls, calm and magnanimous, who do good to others quietly as does the spring, and who having themselves crossed this dreadful ocean of birth and death spontaneously help others also to cross the same.
>
> (Vc. 37)

At the instruction of his guru Govindapada, Shankara, then a young boy of twelve, came to Varanasi (Benares), an ancient seat of the Vedic religion and culture, and began teaching in public. Here his first monastic disciple, Sanandana (afterwards known as Padmapada), one of the chosen four, joined him. As a personal attendant he was closest to Shankara. Gradually other disciples came.

After staying in Varanasi for some time, Shankara travelled on foot with his disciples all the way to Hardwar, and from Hardwar to Badarikashrama, a place of pilgrimage near the source of the Alakananda, a tributary of the Bhagirathi (the main stream of the Ganges), in the high

Himalayan altitudes. On his way from Varanasi Shankara visited every notable sacred place and worshipped the Deity in the temple, setting an example for the followers of the path of devotion, and demonstrating at the same time that a knower of Nirguna Brahman (the Impersonal Absolute) is not devoid of devotion to Saguna Brahman, the Personal God.

According to Advaita Vedanta only highly qualified spiritual aspirants can follow the path of knowledge, the direct approach to Nirguna Brahman. Others have to realize Saguna Brahman along the path of devotion before they can reach the Nirguna.

At Badarikashrama Shankara stayed about three years and wrote his most important works — the commentaries on 1) the ten principal Upanishads, 2) the *Brahma-sutras*, and 3) the *Bhagavad-gita* — the triple basis of the religion and philosophy of Vedanta. Then he visited other holy places in the Himalayas.

Shankara was by now past sixteen. He travelled all over India, propagating the Vedic teachings. After completing his tour in Southern India as far as the temple of Rameswara Shiva near the southern-most point of India, he turned northwards and travelled throughout the length and breadth of the country, revisiting many of the holy places. At every notable place he explained the Advaita position and invited its opponents of the Vedic as well as of the non-Vedic schools to open debate. In most places people came to him for enlightenment and guidance, for the solution of their problems, and for the discussion of their views with him.

He prescribed religious courses according to the

worshipper's inner development and situation in life. He stressed the performance of duties according to the social status (varna) and the stage of life (ashrama). He wanted to reform the social order by reforming the lives of the individuals without any revolutionary attempt.

In many places Shankara established not only monasteries and temples, but also Sanskrit academies for the Vedic culture. Besides the commentaries on the Upanishads, the *Brahma-sutras*, and the *Bhagavad-gita*, he wrote a number of valuable guide-books, both in prose and poetry, for the seekers of Self-knowledge. He also composed many poems and hymns in praise of Shiva, Vishnu and Shakti. He stressed the worship of the Personal God especially in these three aspects.

Shankara was as great a poet as a prose-writer. His poetry is remarkable for its sublimity of thought and devotional fervor. His style is fluent and rhythmical; his language is marked by profundity and clarity. About twenty-two commentaries, seventy-five hymns and poems, and fifty-four guide-books and primers are assigned to him. Shankara was a versatile genius: a mystic, a saint, a philosopher, a polemist, an indefatigable reformer, and a literary man of the highest order.

After twenty years intense work for the revival of the Vedic religion throughout India, Shankara came to Kedarnath for the second and last time. He was now in his thirty-second year. He knew that the term of his life was going to expire. But something was yet to be done for the continuity of the work. For the cultivation and the dissemination of spiritual knowledge under monastic guidance he had planned the foundation of four principal monasteries (maths) at four cardinal points of India — at Sringeri (near Rameswara) in the south; at Puri (on the Bay of Bengal) in the east; at Dwarka (on the Arabian Sea) in the west; and at Yoshi in the North (in the Himalayas). Each monastery was meant to be under the leadership of one of his four chief disciples, and to be the custodian of one of the four Vedas. India was to be divided into four sections — southern, eastern, western, and northern — each under the jurisdiction of one of the four monasteries. Being aware of his approaching end, Shankara called his disciples to his side and told them about his plan.

The monastery at Sringeri had already been established by him with Suresharacharya as its head. Now he assigned to Padmapada the leadership of the Govardhan Math at Puri; Hastamalaka the leadership of the Sarada Math at Dwarka; and Totakacharya the leadership of the Jyotir Math at Yoshi in the Himalayas. He also decided that the Yajur-Veda was to be taken care of by Sringeri Math; the Rig-Veda by Govardhan Math; the Sama-Veda by Sarada Math; and the Atharva-Veda by Jyotir Math. The head of each monastery was to promote both by example and precept the spiritual well-being of the laity as well as of the monastics within his jurisdiction. Shankara also drew up certain regulations for the guidance of the monasteries. At Kedarnath, the mountain-top sacred to Shiva and guarded by snow-clad peaks, he left the body in mahasamadhi.

Shankaracharya reorganized the ancient monastic order under ten different denominations: Giri, Puri, Bharati, Saraswati, Vana, Aranya, Tirtha, Ashrama, Parbata and Sagara. Saraswati, Puri and Bharati are associated with Sringeri Math; Vana and Aranya with

Govardhan Math; Tirtha, Ashrama and Giri with Sarada Math; Parbata and Sagara with Jyotir Math.

Shankara's exposition of Nondualistic (Advaita) Vedanta is accepted as authoritative for three main reasons:

1. His sound knowledge of the scriptures;
2. His rationality; and
3. His experience of Nondual Brahman in nirvikalpa samadhi.

Consequently, it can be assumed that his predecessors whose texts on Nondualistic Vedanta have been counted as authoritative must have had these three assets. For instance, Gaudapada, the preceptor of Shankara's preceptor, Govindapada, wrote a versified exposition of two hundred and fifteen couplets on the *Mandukya Upanishad*, the shortest of all the Upanishads. Shankara wrote his first commentary on Gaudapada's *Mandukya-Karika* and concluded with an obeisance to Gaudapada, his grand-preceptor. Ananda-Giri wrote his gloss on Shankara's commentary on the *Karika* just as he wrote his gloss on Shankara's other commentaries.[1]

Indeed, Gaudapada's *Karika* is the pioneer work on Advaita Vedanta during the revival of the Vedic religion on the decline of Buddhism. Shankara was full of reverence to Gaudapada. All this testifies to the fact that Gaudapada was not only possessed of the knowledge of the Sruti and reasoning power but was also an experiencer of Nondual Brahman. Indeed, *Karika* No. 80, Chap. 4, is reminiscent of Gaudapada's status. It runs as follows:

---

[1]See Ananda Ashrama Sanskrit Series #10 *Gaudapada-Karika* with the commentary of Shankara and the gloss of Ananda-Giri.

> When the mind turns away from dualities and is not occupied with them any more because of their non-existence, that is the attainment of Brahman, nondual and eternal.

On the other hand, Govindapada, though an experiencer of Nondual Brahman, is not known to have written any Vedantic treatise. From this we can infer that there have been other great knowers of Brahman who did not produce any literary work, whose names are not recorded in history.

The earliest instances of the knowers of Nondual Brahman we find in the *Rig-Veda Samhita*. The *Chhandogya Upanishad* (which belongs to the *Sama-Veda Samhita*) concludes Chapter 3, Section 17, with two significant quotations from the *Rig-Veda Samhita*.

> They (the knowers of Brahman) see everywhere the Supreme Light, which shines in Brahman, which is all-pervading like the light of day, and which derives from the Source of the universe.[2]
>
> Perceiving the higher light (in the sun) which removes the darkness (of ignorance) as the higher light in the heart, and thus (perceiving the Supreme Light) which is higher than all lights, we have reached the highest Light, the Sun, the most luminous among the gods. Yea, we have reached the highest Light, the Sun, the most luminous among the gods.[3]

---

[2]Mandala 8, Sukta 30, *Rig-Veda Samhita* (text with exhaustive index). Edited by Sreepada Sarma Satavalekara, Svadhyaya-mandala, Paradi, Surat, India.

[3]Mandala 1, Suktas 10, 11. Ibid.

Evidently in the passages quoted above the *Rig-Veda Samhita* delineates the states of the illumined ones who live after the realization of the identity of the individual self with the Supreme Self in nirvikalpa samadhi, that is to say, after the realization of Nirguna Brahman. They are regarded as living-free personages (jivanmukta purushas). In the same *Chhandogya Upanishad* we notice another quotation which refers to the living-free personage.

> The seer does not see death or disease or sorrow. The seer sees everything and obtains everything everywhere [because he realizes the all-pervading Self].
>
> (Ch.U. VII:26.2)

In the *Rig-Veda Samhita* we also find the self-declaration of the sage Vamadeva[4] and also of Vachaknavi,[5] the daughter of the sage Ambhrina, which are evidences of their being living-free souls. They declare the identity of the indwelling self with the Self that dwells in all. This view is corroborated by the *Brihadaranyaka Upanishad.*[6]

Coming down to the Upanishadic age, we find some instances of the knowers of Brahman. The sage Svetasvatara declares his realization of the identity of the witness-self with the all-pervading Supreme Self (Brahman):

[4] *Rig-Veda* — Mandala IV:26.1-3. See *Rig-Veda Samhita* with the commentary of Sayanacharya edited by F. Max Muller, Vol. II, p. 424.

[5] *Rig-Veda* — Mandala X:125.1-8 (Vak-sukta). *Ibid.* Vol. IV, p. 412.

[6] In Br.U. I:4.10, there is reference to Vamadeva: "The seer Vamadeva, having realized this [self] as That, came to know: 'I was Manu and the sun.' And to this day, whoever in a like manner knows the self as 'I am Brahman,' becomes all this [universe]. Even the gods cannot prevent his becoming this, for he has become their self."

I have realized this Supreme Being who shines effulgent like the sun beyond all darkness. One passes beyond death only on realizing Him. There is no other way of escape from the cycles of birth and rebirth.

There is naught superior or inferior to That; naught smaller or greater than That. Rooted in His own glory He stands firm like a tree, One without a second and immovable. By That Being the whole universe is filled.[7]

In the *Chhandogya Upanishad* we find how the sage Uddalaka instructed his son, Svetaketu, on the way of Self-knowledge by various illustrations. The instruction continued as follows:

Just as someone, my dear, might lead a person, with his eyes covered, away from [his native place — the country of] the Gandharas, and leave him in a place where there were no human beings; and just as that person would turn toward the east, or the north, or the south, or the west, shouting: 'I have been brought here with my eyes covered, I have been left here with my eyes covered!'

And as thereupon someone might loosen the covering and say to him: 'Gandhara is in that direction; go that way'; and as thereupon, having been informed and being capable of judgment, he would by asking his way from one village to another, arrive at last at Gandhara — in exactly the same manner does a man who has found a teacher to instruct him obtain the true knowledge. For him there is delay only so long as he is not liberated [from the body]; then he reaches perfection.[8]

In conclusion, the sage Uddalaka said to Svetaketu:

[7]Sv.U. III:8,9.
[8]Ch.U. VI:14.1,2.

> Now, that which is the subtle essence — in it all that
> exists has its self. That is the True. That is the Self. That
> thou art, Svetaketu.[9]

As you notice, the terse sentence "That thou art"
declaring the identity of the individual self with the Supreme
Self, is a Mahavakya. Evidently the sage Uddalaka was a
knower of Nondual Brahman.

In the same *Chhandogya Upanishad,* we find another
instance of a knower of Nondual Brahman. It is the sage
Sanatkumara. Narada, after having studied all the Vedas,
including all the subsidiary studies, approached
Sanatkumara in order to go beyond all sorrow.
Sanatkumara imparted to him, by gradual stages, the
knowledge of Brahman, which removed all his sorrow and
filled him with Bliss Infinite. The knower of Brahman also
leads his adherent to the Goal.

From the *Brihadaranyaka Upanishad*, we get the
impression that the sage Yajnavalkya was recognized by his
contemporaries as a knower of Brahman, a man of
realization.

Following the Upanishadic age is the age of the
Brahma-sutras. The Upanishads consist mainly of the
suprasensuous truths revealed to the mystic vision of the
seers, who declare what they see. They do not, as a rule,
argue or reason. Speculation is not their way. In course of
time there arose the necessity of systematizing the
Upanishadic statements in order to resolve their apparent
contradictions and to convey their import in terms of

[9]Ch.U. VI:16.3.

reason. The transcendental truths, although beyond the reach of reason, admit of rational interpretation. Otherwise they cannot be universally accepted.

Several attempts were made from the earliest days to present the Upanishadic truths in terms of reason, but none of these treatises is available in the present age except Badarayana Vyasa's *Brahma-sutras.* This forms the basis of Vedanta as rational philosophy, and is highly esteemed as authoritative by all schools of Vedanta — the monistic (nondualistic) and the monotheistic. The treatise consists altogether of 555 sutras or aphorisms.

While the Upanishads constitute the mystical and the *Brahma-sutras* the rational basis of Vedanta, the *Bhagavad-gita* dwells on the problem of the application of the Upanishadic truths to active life. It forms the third stage of Vedanta — that of applied truths. These three — the Upanishads, the *Brahma-sutras*, and the *Bhagavad-gita*, are respectively known as the *Sruti-prasthana*, the *Nyaya-prasthana*, and the *Smriti-prasthana* Vedanta, inasmuch as they follow the way of revelation, of reason, and of regulation of life, indicated by the terms *Sruti, Nyaya,* and *Smriti,* respectively. All the schools of Vedanta including the five monotheistic schools of Vaishnavism are grounded on this triple foundation. Thus we find that in the system of Vedanta, mysticism is harmonized with rationality, and the philosophy of life is allied with the way of life.

The later development of Hindu scriptures has taken place on this triple basis: 1) The Upanishads, 2) The *Brahma-sutras,* 3) The *Bhagavad-gita.* They come under four main heads:

1. The *Puranas* — which aim to impart spiritual teachings mainly by anecdotes, legendary and historical. There are eighteen puranas, such as the *Brahma Purana; Bhagavat Purana; Vishnu Purana; Agni Purana.*

2. *Smritis* — moral and social codes for the guidance of the people in general. No less than twenty of them exist, such as *Manu Smriti; Yajnavalkya Smriti; Parasara Smriti.*

3. The two great epics — the *Ramayana* and the *Mahabharata* — based mainly on historical facts. They specially depict the lives and deeds of the heroes.

4. The *Tantras* dealing with religious rites and practices of the Vaishnavas, the Shaivas, and the Shaktas. Of these *Narada-Pancharatra* is widely known.

As a rule, the leaders of Hindu religions have made earnest efforts to develop the lives of followers in general at different levels. Besides the original texts, there were expository treatises. Many of them are extinct. References to them are found in extant literature.

Since the time of Badarayana Vyasa, the author of the *Brahma-sutras*, each religious and philosophical school has produced a number of treatises, original texts, commentaries and sub-commentaries. Many of these are no longer available.

There are hardly any references to the authors' personal lives in their writings. Consequently we know very little about them and their spiritual caliber. It can be easily surmised that they dedicated their lives to propagate the spiritual truths for the benefit of the earnest seekers.

We do have a definite account of the development of Advaita philosophy from the time of Gaudapada. Advaita Vedanta treatises including the original texts, commentaries and sub-commentaries have flourished continuously from his time through Shankara and his followers, down to the close of the seventeenth century. We know their merit through their works. However, we have very little knowledge of their lives and still less of their spiritual attainments.

Without being far from truth we can conclude that the greatest of these advocates of Advaita Vedanta was Madhusudana Saraswati, who lived approximately from the middle of the 16th to the middle of the 17th century. His contributions cover a very vast field, and include *Advaita-siddhi*, a monumental work on Advaita philosophy, which establishes Shankara's nondualism on a secure foundation by thoroughly refuting all the charges levelled against it by Vyasacharya (a follower of Madhvacharya) in his *Nyaya-mrita*. Besides, he wrote commentaries on the *Bhagavad-gita, Samksepa-sariraka, Srimad Bhagavatam, Nirvana-desakam, Atma-bodha, Shiva-mahimna-stotra,* etc. His extensive commentary on Shankara's *Nirvana-desakam* (Ten Slokas on Nirvana) is well-known as *Siddhanta Vindu.* His original works are *Bhakti-rasayana, Prasthana-bheda, Advaita-ratna-raksana, Vedanta-kalpalatika,* etc.

In Benares he studied Advaita Vedanta under Swami Rama Tirtha. He was initiated into monastic life by Swami Visveswara Saraswati. From what little we know about his life and contributions to Advaita Vedanta we can surmise that he had realized both Saguna and Nirguna Brahman.

However, it is worthy of note, apart from the literary field, that the cultivation of spiritual life according to the Advaita ideal has continued in an unbroken line of teachers and disciples successively from the earliest days down to the modern age. Although their names are unknown, some of them must have realized either Nirguna or Saguna Brahman, or both.

A glaring instance of the realization of Nirguna Brahman in nirvikalpa samadhi in this modern age we find in the life of Sri Ramakrishna, as recorded by his direct disciple Swami Saradananda.

It was Tota Puri, who owed allegiance to the Sringeri Math,[10] the custodian of *Yajur-Veda* to which the *Brihadaranyaka Upanishad* belongs, who happened to be at Dakshineswar in the course of his pilgrimages. He initiated Sri Ramakrishna into the monastic life, and imparted to him the knowledge of the identity of the individual self with the Supreme Self, and enabled him to realize Nirguna Brahman in nirvikalpa samadhi.

In the words of Sri Ramakrishna as recorded by Swami Saradananda,

" 'After initiating me,' said the Master, 'the naked one[11] taught me many dicta conveying the conclusion of the Vedanta, and asked me to make my mind free of function in all respects and merge in the meditation of the Self. But, it so happened with me that when I sat for meditation I could by no means make my mind go beyond the bounds of name and form and cease functioning. The mind withdrew itself easily from all other things, but as soon as it did so, the intimately

---

[10]For the ten denominations of the monastic order associated with the four monasteries founded by Shankara, see pp. 222-223.

[11]Since Tota Puri used only a loin cloth, Sri Ramakrishna endearingly called him "the naked one."

familiar form of the universal Mother, consisting of the effulgence of Pure Consciousness, appeared before it as living and moving and made me quite oblivious of the renunciation of names and forms of all descriptions. When I listened to the conclusive dicta and sat for meditation, this happened over and over again. Almost despairing of the attainment of the nirvikalpa samadhi, I then opened my eyes and said to the naked one,"No, it cannot be done; I cannot make the mind free from functioning and force it to dive into the Self." '

" 'Scolding me severely, the naked one said very excitedly, "What, it can't be done! What utter defiance!" He then looked about in the hut and finding a broken piece of glass he took it in his hand and forcibly pierced its needle-like pointed end into my forehead between the eyebrows and said, "Collect the mind here to this point." With a firm determination I sat for meditation; and again, as soon as the holy form of the Divine Mother appeared now before the mind as previously, I looked upon knowledge as a sword and cut it mentally in two with that sword of knowledge. There remained then no function in the mind, which transcended quickly the realm of names and forms, making me merge in samadhi.'

"Sri Tota," says Swami Saradananda, "remained sitting for a long time beside the Master who entered into samadhi in the manner mentioned before. Then coming out of the hut silently, he locked the door up lest someone should enter the hut without his knowledge and disturb him. He took his seat under the Panchavati, not far from the hut and was awaiting the Master's call to open the door.

"The day passed into night. Slowly and calmly days

rolled on. At the end of three days, when Tota did not still hear the Master's call, he was filled with curiosity and astonishment and left his seat to open the door. With a view to knowing the condition of his disciple, he entered the hut and saw that the Master was sitting in the same posture in which he had left him and that there was not the slightest function of the vital force in his body, but that his face was calm and serene and full of effulgence. He understood that the disciple was completely dead to the external world and that his mind, merged in Brahman, was calm and motionless like an unflickering lamp in a windless place. ...

"Tota then undertook the process of bringing the disciple back to the consciousness of the external world. Profound sounds of the mantra 'Hari Aum' filled the land, water and sky of the Panchavati."[12]

Gradually Sri Ramakrishna's mind descended to the normal level of consciousness.

Sri Ramakrishna's life was a complete demonstration of both nirvikalpa and savikalpa samadhi. Throughout the rest of his life he had almost daily experiences of the one or the other, or both.

Once being asked about the nature of Sri Ramakrishna's samadhi Swami Brahmananda, his most intimate and beloved disciple, said, "He remained absorbed in different states of samadhi at different times." Indeed, the Divine Master was capable of moving up and down the different stages of ecstatic experience from its acme in nirvikalpa samadhi to the varying devotional moods with more or less external consciousness. This was due to the fact

[12]*Great Master,* pp.255-56.

that the usual resting ground of his mind was somewhere between Nirguna and Saguna Brahman, the line of demarcation of the Absolute and the relative, whence all individuations proceed. This is technically called *bhava-mukha,* the starting-point of all ideations.

Usually he daily experienced both nirvikalpa and savikalpa samadhi. In the normal state he always perceived the all-pervading Self. The resting ground of his "I" consciousness was the Supreme Self. Besides experiencing samadhi himself, he had the power to lift the inner consciousness of the disciples to the state of samadhi according to their capabilities. Narendranath, later Swami Vivekananda, attained nirvikalpa samadhi, and other disciples attained savikalpa samadhi under Sri Ramakrishna's guidance and inspiration.

In nirvikalpa samadhi, Sri Ramakrishna's "I-consciousness" disappeared totally; his pulse, heart-beat, etc., stopped simultaneously. Sri Mahendralal Sarkar and other doctors examined him with the help of instruments and found no sign of the functioning of his heart. Not satisfied with that, his friend, another doctor, went further and touched with his finger the Master's eyeball, and found it insensitive to touch like that of a dead man.

There was no indication of life except the warmth of the body, which is maintained by Udana Vayu according to the Vedantic conception of the five vital forces and which is the last to leave the body.[13]

"Firmly established in the plane of the nondual

[13]Prana, Apana, Samana, Vyana, Udana. Udana maintains the heat in the body and is the last to leave the body. It functions when all the other vital forces stop functioning.

consciousness," as pointed out by Swami Saradananda, "the Master had the realization of another fact also. He came to feel in his heart of hearts that the realization of nonduality was the ultimate aim of all kinds of sadhanas. For, having performed sadhanas according to the teachings of all the main religious denominations prevalent in Bharata [India], he had already been convinced that they all took the aspirants towards the nondual plane."[14]

[14]*Great Master,* p. 262.

PART THREE

Appendices

From Mortality to Immortality*

There is no denying that man is mortal. Not only is he subject to death, but each and every living thing must die. In this world of uncertainties, death is the only settled fact. Yet no one knows how death will come, nor where, nor when. No place is secure from death. No measure of caution can avert death.

Death has no regard for anything in this universe. No position, be it intellectual, physical, moral, or even spiritual is immune from it. Yet the human mind refuses to accept death as something final, and we find the sages of the world declaring that death of the body is not the end of an individual's existence.

The physical body dies and disintegrates, but the spirit that passes out of the body continues to exist. As long as a person is considered only a physical being, death is thought to be his end; but man is not just a physical or psychophysical being, he is a spiritual entity. This is what the scriptures declare.

Our common sense, also, cannot accept death as the final end of an individual. It leaves human life completely

*First printed in *Vedanta and the West,* March-April, 1969, 196:28-36.

meaningless and unexplained. If death were the end of existence, then our sense of justice is frustrated, our labor is unrewarded, and our desires and aspirations are unrealized. Human reason, human feeling cannot accept death as final.

Why should mortal man have such a deep-seated yearning for immortality? There must be some explanation for it. There is a story from the *Mahabharata* concerning the Pandava princes. These five brothers were living in a forest in exile. One day after walking a long distance, they felt very thirsty. The youngest brother was sent in search of water. He found a beautiful lake and was going to drink the water, when he heard a voice say, "I am the presiding deity of this lake, first answer my questions, and then drink." But the brother did not listen; he sipped just a little water, and promptly fell dead.

Meanwhile the other brothers wondered what had happened and another brother was sent to search. He found the lake and saw his brother lying dead, close to the water's edge. This brother also wanted a drink and as he bent down the same voice spoke out, "I am the presiding deity of this water. First answer my questions, and then drink." But he could not stop to answer the questions and as he sipped the water he too fell dead. The third and fourth brothers went to the lake and met the same fate.

Finally, the fifth brother, Yudhisthira, went to the lake, and saw his four brothers lying there. The same voice spoke to him, and appeared in the form of a *yaksa* (demi-god), the god of justice. The yaksa said, "Answer my questions and then drink this water."

"What are the questions?" asked Yudhisthira.

The yaksa asked him many questions, which the young

sage duly answered. Finally he was asked, "What is the most wonderful fact of life?"

Yudhisthira replied, "Each and every one is subject to death. Men and women are dying by the thousands, yet those who remain behind believe themselves to be out of death's reach. This is the most wonderful fact in the world."

Yes, death comes to all, but all cling to life. Thus the Vedantic scriptures explain the immortality of the spirit.

In every case of perception there are two distinct factors. One is the object of perception, the other is the perceiver. What is the difference between the object of perception and the perceiver? We must remember that the existence of an object always presupposes the existence of a perceiver. It is the perceiver who establishes the reality of the object perceived. But we ignore the perceiver and accept the objective universe as real in itself, forgetting the necessity for a subject in order that an object can exist. The one fundamental difference between the object perceived and the perceiver is this: the perceiver is self-aware. The object has no inherent consciousness.

Similarly, Vedanta says that this distinction between the object and the subject holds good with regard to the human personality as well. Just as an external object is perceived, so is this physical body an object of perception. An individual knows himself to be either dark or fair, sick or healthy; or whether his body is growing or decaying.

The body is an object of perception, and so is the mind an object of perception. Just as one can watch external events, so can one watch the movements of the mind. Mental phenomena are observed by that same perceiver. And there is a vital difference between the spirit that perceives the mind, the body, the senses, and the objects perceived.

The spirit is always there whether the object is there or not. This whole universe, for instance, drops from your consciousness when you dream. There is an altogether different order of perceived objects and perceived facts in the dream state. Yet, the same perceiver is persistently there; but the objects perceived are changing. When deep sleep is experienced, there is no feeling, no memory, no thought; still, the perceiver is there. The same experiencer says, "I slept, I did not know anything. I dreamt, I slept, I awoke." This means that all the objects of perception belonging to this physical body and the mind are changing, but the perceiver is enduring and changeless. The external objects change, the body changes, the senses change, the mind changes, but the perceiver is constant. This is the one factor that never changes. It reveals your dream state, your sleep state and waking state, but is separate from all of these.

So through reasoning one can become convinced that a person is not only distinct from external objects, but separate from his own physical body and ever-changing mind. While the external objects — the body, senses, and mind — are bereft of consciousness, one always has consciousness within him. This is the same in sleep, in dream, or in the waking state, and this consciousness maintains our identity.

Our body may change, our thoughts and ideas may be revolutionized; still, we say that we are the same. "I was playing around my grandfather's knees; now I have grandchildren playing around my knees." Think of this! The mind and body have completely changed! A person may not even recognize himself in a photograph taken when he was a child; still he knows that he was that child.

What maintains our individuality? Underlying all these changing factors, there is a perceiver which is of the nature of Pure Consciousness. It is changeless; and at the same time blissful, because it is always loved. And because it is loved, everything identified with it is loved. The house is dear, the children are dear, even the clothes one wears are dear because they are related to this Self, this Perceiver. That Self is pure, luminous, constant, changeless, and blissful. This is its nature, and it is ever-present.

Yet, just as fire is covered with smoke, this spirit is covered with a kind of ignorance. An individual fails to realize his true nature as pure spirit. He not only fails to do this, but he identifies himself with this body-mind and thus becomes young or old, healthy or sick, ignorant or wise, simply through the identification of the pure spirit with this body and psychophysical system. As long as he does this he cannot be immortal in the true sense. For example, a person may have some money in his purse, but if he is not aware of it he may as well be poor. Similarly, so long as a person does not realize his real self as being pure spirit, he will remain mortal.

It is said in the Upanishads that like corn, human beings die and decay. After death, a person may have another body, but he will die again. Why do people die? Because they are born. Anything that has a beginning, anything that is born, must die. This is an inevitable truth.

Suppose the physical body is revived after having undergone death. Will not that make a person immortal? No, for death will come again. It is said that Sri Krishna restored to life the son of his teacher Sandipani. Jesus Christ restored Lazarus to life. But where are they now? Restoration of the dead body does not mean immortality, here or hereafter.

A person can attain immortality even while living by realizing his identity with the immortal spirit and the fact that this spirit is separate from the body. "Death, where is thy sting?" said St. Paul. He knew that the body would die, yet he knew that he was an immortal spirit. There have been sages and seers who have realized the immortal spirit, and they defied death.

One story has been common in India for a long time. When Alexander the Great invaded India, he came as far as the river Indus. He was a great patron of learning and a lover of wise men, and he had heard of an Indian sage living nearby. He found this sage and requested him to return to Macedonia with him. The sage replied, "I am quite happy here, I need not go anywhere."

Alexander tried to persuade him in different ways, but when the saint said firmly, "No. I shall remain here," Alexander drew his sword and said, "Then I shall kill you."

The sage laughed and replied, "You have never spoken so foolishly. How can you kill me? Weapons cannot pierce me, fire cannot burn me, water cannot wet me, air cannot dry me. I am immortal."

If an individual fails to realize the immortality of the spirit, he is mortal. Realization of our eternal nature can be effected in two ways. First, by reasoning about it; second, by meditating upon this truth and thus attaining the realization of God. In Vedanta, God-realization and Self-realization are not distinct. In trying to realize your spiritual Self, you realize God, because God is the Soul of your soul. As Christ said, "The Kingdom of Heaven is within you."

In realizing God, then, you realize your self. In realizing the Self, you realize God. Thus Sri Ramakrishna remarked if a person can know himself in the true sense, he will know God. There is a kinship between the human spirit and the Divine Spirit, and when an individual realizes the true nature of his conscious self, he realizes that he belongs to the Supreme Spirit. Just as each and every wave belongs to the ocean, and each and every ray of light belongs to the sun, similarly, each and every soul belongs to God or the Infinite Soul.

We read in the Upanishads: "This form [the form of the Supreme Spirit] does not stand within the range of sense-perception. No one perceives Him with the eye; those who know him through intuition, that mystical awareness, as seated in the heart, become immortal. He lies hidden; Him the cosmic being knows as the source of Himself; those gods and seers who realized Him became identified with Him, and verily became immortal."

And one of the seers declares, "Hear Me, O ye children of immortal bliss, ye that dwell on this earth, ye that dwell in other spheres; hear me. I have realized that Supreme Being, ever resplendent, being of the nature of Pure Consciousness, the Light of all lights, resplendent as the sun, self-effulgent. I know that I belong to Him, and not to this physical universe. Since I have known this truth, I am beyond death — this is the only way to immortality, there is no other way out of the realm of death."

When one approaches the Supreme Being with devotion and worships Him, the mind will become purified. Then one will realize his spiritual nature and eventually realize his self and his essential unity with Divinity.

That Supreme Spirit can be contacted through one's own inner spirit. Whether one tries to realize the Self as distinct from the body, the senses, and the mind; or whether one gradually becomes aware of the true nature of the Self, it is spirit that contacts Spirit. Each and every kind of perception has its own instrument. For the perception of physical forms there are the eyes; for the perception of sounds there are ears; for the perception of mental ideas, there is the mind. Similarly, for the experience of pure spirit there is the spiritual Self. As one becomes aware of the spiritual Self within, God comes closer and closer as the Soul of one's soul, and ultimately one realizes his essential oneness with Him. We read in the *Bhagavad-gita:*

> This Self is never born, nor does it die. It is not that having been it again ceases to be. Even as a man casts out worn-out clothes, and puts on others which are new, so the embodied self casts out worn-out bodies, and enters into others which are new.
>
> This Self weapons cut not, fire burns not, water wets not, wind dries not. This Self cannot be cut, nor burnt, nor wetted, nor dried; changeless, all-pervading, unmoving, unmoved, the Self is eternal.
>
> (B.G. II:20,22-24)

The difference between mortality and immortality, the difference between death and deathlessness is to realize that man's pure Spirit is deathless and immortal, self-luminous consciousness, ever pure, free, and one with the Supreme Spirit.

The Location of the Soul
in the Body

The physical body is called *Brahmapura,* the city of Brahman,[1] because He, the Supreme Being, dwells here as the internal ruler with a retinue of attendants, such as the ten organs (indriyas),[2] the mind (manas),[3] the intellect (buddhi), and so forth. His abode is the lotus of the heart. It is true that Nondual Brahman, Pure Consciousness, the finest of all existences, is immanent in the whole universe as the Omnipresent Being (purusha); but His direct manifestation in the phenomenal world is the innermost self of every individual shining in the depth of the heart. Any expression of consciousness in man's psychophysical system is but a

[1]Ch.U. VIII:1.1.

[2]Ten indriyas — five organs of perception: the eyes, the ears, the nose, the palate, and the skin; the five organs of action: the tongue (organ of speech), the hands, the legs, the organ of evacuation, and the organ of generation.

[3]The term *manas* is also used for the entire mind (antahkarana, lit. the inner instrument or organ). It is to be noted that Hindu psychology distinguishes the cognitive aspect of antahkarana from the volitional and the emotional aspect. Strictly speaking, the cognitive aspect has four different functions: deliberation, determination, egoism, and recollection, called respectively manas, buddhi, ahamkara [egoism], and chitta. The cognitive aspect is primary.

reflection of the luminous self within.

As defined by Shankara: "The heart is a lump of flesh shaped like a lotus-bud facing downwards with the stalk upwards, in which are apertures for numerous arteries, which is the receptacle of life and is familiar, being observed when the body is dissected."[4] Within the heart there is a space about the size of the thumb, where the mind (antahkarana) is located. Hindu psychology stresses two distinct phases of the cognitive mind (antahkarana): the determinative and the deliberative. The one is called buddhi and the other manas. Buddhi is higher than manas. It underlies all determinate knowledge, feeling, and volition. Being constituted preeminently of sattva, buddhi is the finest and purest of all the aspects or modes of the mind. It has the special capacity to transmit or reflect Pure Consciousness immanent in the universe, so to speak, and is similar to a glass sheet that transmits sunlight, or a mirror that reflects the sun.

It is through the mind (antahkarana), particularly through buddhi, that the radiance of Brahman becomes manifest in the psychophysical system. Though located in the heart, the mind can expand and pervade the whole body. The sattva aspects of the five subtle elements[5] being combined produce the mind and because of the essence of sattva the mind has the capacity to reflect the light of consciousness.

Being associated with buddhi (the cognitive aspect of the mind), all-pervading Consciousness becomes identified

---

[4]Commentary on Tai. U. 1:6.
[5]Color or form; taste or flavor; smell; touch; and sound.

with it and seemingly limited. Thus arises the individual self, the witness-self that perceives all changes without undergoing any changes. Being further associated with the ego, a mode of antahkarana, it turns into knower and doer.

Infinite Consciousness appears as the ego. It is the Supreme Self that dwells within the heart as the individual self. The following description of the self bears out this point:

> Which is the self? This Omnipresent Being (purusha) that is identified with buddhi and is in the midst of the organs, the [self-effulgent] light within the heart.
>
> (Br.U. IV:3.7)

The primary meaning of "the heart" is the lotus-shaped lump of flesh. Here it signifies buddhi, a phase of the cognitive aspect of the mind, which is located in the heart. Buddhi is the most refined of all the modifications of prakriti that constitute man's psychophysical system. It is but natural that it should have its seat in the heart, the central and most vital part of the body, and be the fit instrument for the manifestation of atman. Indeed, the heart is the true abode of man's innermost self, the center of his personality. This is also evidenced by the fact that an individual spontaneously points to the heart, while referring to himself or herself.

Further, the seekers of Truth, free from worldly desires, with their senses withdrawn and their minds purified, realize Brahman as directly as a plum in the palm of the hand by constantly meditating on the luminous self within the heart as the all-pervading Supreme Self. So it is said: "In this city of Brahman there is a small lotus, an abode. Inside this there is a tiny space (akasha). That which is within this, one should seek and yearn to know."[6]

The self is said to be identified with buddhi (the cognitive aspect), because of man's failure to discriminate it from this limiting adjunct. Being mixed up they seemingly partake of each other's nature. On the one hand, the self, which is intrinsically Pure Consciousness, appears to be endowed with the characteristics of buddhi, such as knowledge, determination, volition, and so forth; in the same way as light shining through glass appears red, green, or blue according to the color of the glass. On the other hand, buddhi, which is material, appears as intelligent being permeated by consciousness, just as glass appears radiant in association with light. The identification of the self with buddhi leads to its identification with all else.

> This self is indeed that Brahman identified with buddhi, with manas, with prana (the life-principle), with the eyes, with the ears, with earth, with water, with air, with fire and what is other than fire, with desire and absence of desire, with virtue and absence of virtue, with everything, with this [what is perceived] and with that [what is inferred].
>
> (Br.U. IV:4.5)

The individual self is said to be of the size of the thumb, because the space inside the heart, wherein it is manifest, is very small. Freed from its limiting adjuncts the indwelling self is the all-pervading Brahman, formless and featureless. So it is said:

[6]Ch.U. VIII:1.1.

The Omnipresent Being (purusha), as the innermost self of the size of the thumb, ever exists in the hearts of men. Him should man carefully distinguish from his [threefold] body like the slender stalk from munja grass. Him should man know as effulgent and immortal; Him should man know as effulgent and immortal.

(Ka.U. II:3.17)

It is the light of the self shining through buddhi that reveals whatever we experience. So says Shankara:

Buddhi is the instrument for the perception of all objects like a lamp placed in front amid darkness. It has been said, "It is through the mind that one sees, that one hears." Indeed, everything is perceived on being invested with the light of buddhi like an object in the dark illuminated by a lamp placed in front. The other organs are but the channels of buddhi.[7]

It is true that without external light nothing can be seen; but external light helps the eyes only when they are associated with consciousness. This is why a person cannot see things even in daylight when he is absent-minded, or asleep with the eyes open. The inner light of consciousness proceeding through buddhi and the organ of vision first reveals the external light. Being illuminated by the radiance of consciousness external light manifests things.

All perceptions and all activities of man are due to the radiance of the luminous self permeating the mind, the organs, and the body. The process of permeation of the light of consciousness is thus described by Shankara:

[7]Commentary on Br.U. IV:3.7.

"Buddhi being transparent and nearest to the intelligent self instantly receives the reflection of its radiance. This is why even a man of discrimination identifies himself with it first. Next to that is manas. It receives the radiance of consciousness being associated with buddhi; then the organs, being connected with the mind; then the body, through contact with the organs. Thus the self successively illumines with the radiance of its effulgent being the whole aggregate of the body and the organs. It is because of this that every human being identifies himself with the body and the organs and their functions, in his own way, without any system, according to his understanding.

" So the Lord said in the *Bhagavad-gita:* "As the one sun, O Bharata, lights up the entire world, so the self, the knower of the field of the body, illumines the whole body." . . . Therefore the self is the light within buddhi located in the heart. This is the all-pervading Being, whose self-effulgence is utmost, because He is the illuminator of everything, and not illumined by anything else."[8]

[8]Commentary on Br.U. IV:3.7.

The Sum and Substance
of Advaita Vedanta

According to Nondualistic Vedanta the sum and substance of the Vedantic texts, numerous as they are, is this: "Brahman is real, the world is unreal; the jiva is verily Brahman and no other." Since this statement is very often misunderstood, I shall make an attempt to bring out its significance in accordance with Shankara. I shall dwell on its two parts successively.

1. The meaning of "Brahman is real, the world is unreal."

In declaring the reality of Brahman and the unreality of the world, Advaita Vedanta repudiates the ultimate reality of the world of experience, but not its empirical existence. When the jiva attains illumination and realizes Brahman, the relative order disappears altogether. So, from his standpoint, the world is utterly false. But an unillumined person invariably perceives the phenomenal world and not Brahman. To him, the diversified universe is a fact of experience; it is not false in the sense that the son of a barren woman is false. Nobody ever perceives the son of a barren woman either in reality or in illusion. As long as a person dreams, the dream-world is real to him; dream-water allays his dream-thirst. He knows the dream-world to be unreal only when he wakes up. So says Shankara: "Empirical experiences are valid until the identity of the self with Brahman is realized, as are dream-experiences until awaking."[1]

To be explicit, the world, as characterized by Advaita Vedanta, is neither real nor unreal. It is not real, because it is sublated by the knowledge of Nondual Brahman. Yet it is not unreal, because it is a fact of experience for the unillumined. Thus the world-order can be viewed from the standpoint of the illumined and also from the standpoint of the unillumined. On this twofold world-view, Shankara observes:

"This phenomenal world, caused by diversification and deceptive, is a fact for those who hold that things are different from Brahman and also for those who do not. The adherents of the Supreme Truth, however, while investigating, in accord with the Sruti, the true nature of things (whether they really exist or not), arrive at the conclusion that Brahman alone is, the One without a second, beyond all relativity.

"So there is no contradiction between the two views. We do not maintain the existence of anything but Brahman in the state in which the Supreme Truth is attained, as the Srutis say, 'One only without a second' and 'without interior or exterior.' Nor do we deny in the relative plane of name and form the validity for the ignorant of the empirical facts comprising action, its agent, its instrument, its result, and so

[1]Commentary on B.S. II:1.14.

forth.

"Therefore, the scriptural and the empirical outlooks rest on knowledge and ignorance. So there is no fear of contradiction between them. No school can deny that the existence and the non-existence of the phenomenal world depend on the relative and the absolute standpoint."[2]

Sense-perception and the Sruti may appear mutually contradictory. But they are not. According to Shankara, both are sources of valid knowledge in their respective spheres. The province of the Sruti is the transcendental Reality, which is beyond sense-perception. The suprasensuous cannot be reached by inference even. The reason is that inferential knowledge depends on the knowledge of the invariable concomitance between the thing perceived and the thing inferred, and such a knowledge is lacking in the case in point. Nor can any other means of knowledge dependent on sense-perception acquaint us with the nature of the suprasensuous. Therefore, the Sruti is the only source of knowledge with regard to the transcendental Reality.

Most philosophers and scientists recognize the inherent incapability of perception to probe into the fundamental Reality. Its province is the world of appearance. Sir James Jeans says in his book *Physics and Philosophy:* "Our studies can never put us into contact with reality; we can never penetrate beyond the impressions that reality implants in our minds."[3]

It is with regard to the transcendental Reality that the

---

[2]Commentary on Br.U. III:5.1.

[3]Jeans, James, *Physics and Philosophy,* p.15. MacMillan, New York:1946.

Sruti declares: "There is no diversity whatsoever in This [Brahman]."[4] So it does not contradict sense-knowledge. When one person says, "The sun moves," and another with his astronomical knowledge says, "The sun does not move," the two statements do not contradict each other, but represent two different viewpoints regarding the sun.

Similarly, the two statements, "Man is mortal" and "Man is immortal," mutually contradictory though they appear to be, are true from two different viewpoints, the physical and the spiritual. There is no conflict between them. But the value of either depends on the merit of its standpoint. This is so in all such cases.

The following remarks of Madhusudana Saraswati in his *Advaita-siddhi* (I:18) are to the point: "Only the empirical validity of perception and other allied means of knowledge is a proven fact; that is not controverted by the scriptures (agama). What is controverted is its ultimateness, which is by no means a proven fact. Therefore, there is no conflict between perception and the scriptures (agama)."

The fundamental Reality is the substratum of the world-appearance. In fact, it is Nondual Brahman that appears as the manifold. The world, as it appears, is unreal; but in its essential nature as Brahman the world is absolutely real. So the *Chhandogya Upanishad* says: "Verily all this is Brahman." As the supreme principle immanent in the universe, Brahman is its very basis and being. "From Him all things originate, into Him do they dissolve, and by Him are they sustained."[5]

[4]Br.U. IV:4.19.
[5]Ch.U. III:14.1.

The same nonrelational, nondual Brahman is in relation to the world its originator, sustainer, and absorber. Transcendentally Pure Being-Consciousness-Bliss, Brahman as immanent in the universe is its all-pervading, all-knowing, all-powerful, all-merciful Lord. So says Shankara: "Two kinds of Brahman are stated [in the Upanishads]: the one having as its adjuncts the diversities of the universe, the modifications of name and form; the other, its contrary, completely free from all adjuncts."[6] The one is called *apara* (the lower), the other *para* (the higher). The one is *saguna* (immanent), the other is *nirguna* (transcendent).

2. The identity of the jiva and Brahman explained.

From the position of the jiva, the individual experiencer, the world of experience is real, and so is their supreme Ruler. The existence of the individual soul and the universe presupposes the existence of the supreme Lord, because neither of the two is self-existent or self-sufficient. These three are coexistent and inter-related, but are not on the same grade as manifestations of Brahman. None of the three has a beginning. As pointed out by Shankara, their beginning is untenable.[7]

The supreme Lord is the one Self of all. He holds the universe comprising the living and the non-living. Shankara observes: "To the contemplative, nothing other than the supreme Lord exists. He is manifest in the eightfold form of the unmoving and moving, viz. earth, water, fire, air, ether,

[6]Commentary on B.S. I:1.11.
[7]Commentary on B.S. II:1.36.

the sun, the moon, and the individual soul."[8] In the inanimate, He, who is intrinsically pure Being-Consciousness-Bliss, is manifest only as being; in the animate, He is manifest as consciousness as well. It is He who shines as the conscious self in every individual.

One may pertinently ask: How does the undifferentiated One become differentiated, the Unlimited limited, the Changeless changeiul? The question is possible only from the standpoint of the unillumined, who view the world-appearance as real. The point is, all differentiations, limitations, and changes belong to the realm of appearance. The transcendental Reality only *appears* to be different from what It is, but does not *become* so.

The cause of this appearance, according to Advaita Vedanta, is *maya* (lit. that which measures), a mysterious principle that apparently measures the Immeasurable, diversifies the Undiversified, mutates the Immutable. All transformations are in maya, but are superimposed on Brahman. As is the effect, so is the cause. Just as the world-appearance is neither real nor unreal, so is maya. It rests on Brahman without affecting Him in the least. Brahman associated with maya is the supreme Lord of the universe, its originator, preserver, and absorber. He is also the all-gracious Saviour of the souls. He is the adorable One. Maya serves Him as His power.

According to Advaita Vedanta, maya is true so far as the world-appearance is concerned. It does not inhere in Brahman as an ultimate principle. According to all monotheistic systems of Vedanta, maya, the creative energy

[8]Dm.S. 9.

of God, inheres in Him. It is inseparably connected with His being. Nevertheless, Advaita Vedanta argues that in that case, any changes in maya must mean changes in God Himself and the seed of imperfection of the world must be within Him; so this position is not tenable.

The phenomenal world is real to the individual soul (the jiva), but cannot be reckoned as his creation. The existence of maya, its origin, is a fact from his position. With individual ajnana (ignorance) there must be cosmic maya associated with the supreme Lord (Isvara). The one betokens the other as the fruit betokens the tree. This does not mean, of course, that cosmic maya exists because of individual ajnana. It is individual ajnana that derives from cosmic maya, and not cosmic maya from individual ajnana. Brahman is apparently the locus of both.

Brahman with the adjunct of cosmic maya is Isvara, the supreme Lord; Brahman with the adjunct of individual ajnana is the jiva, the individual soul. Thus the jiva is identical in essence with Isvara. But with their respective adjuncts, they are ever different from one another. By realizing the essential identity with Isvara, the jiva becomes Brahman, what he really is. Verily, the knower of Brahman attains Brahman.

Isvara-hood is invariably linked with jiva-hood. Both are manifestations of Brahman through maya in its cosmic and individual aspects. Isvara is ever related to the jiva as Ruler to the ruled. The one is the supreme object of worship, the other is the worshipper. The jiva can never be Isvara. They are coexistent and without beginning. But neither is ultimate.

As observed by Shankara:

"And He (Isvara) stands in the empirical realm in the relation of the Ruler to the cognizing souls called the jivas, which are really one with His own Self (just as portions of ether inside jars are one with the universal ether), but are limited by the aggregates of the body and the senses made of names and forms brought forth by ajnana. Therefore, the lordship of Isvara, His omniscience, omnipotence, are relative to the finite beings due to limiting adjuncts derived from ajnana; in reality, such expressions as the ruler, the ruled, omniscience, and so forth, do not apply to the Self from whose being all adjuncts are wiped out by right knowledge."[9]

Further he says:

"Moreover, when the consciousness of the identity (of the individual soul with the Supreme Being) is aroused by such instruction of their identity as 'That thou art,' then the finiteness of the individual soul and the creatorship of Brahman vanish at once, because all experience of difference proceeding from wrong knowledge is annihilated by perfect knowledge."[10]

Beyond both jiva-hood and Isvara-hood is the undifferentiated Pure Consciousness that Brahman is. The truth that the Sruti reveals by the terse formula, "That thou art," is confirmed by reason and verified by the seer's experience.

[9]Commentary on B.S. II:1.14.
[10]Commentary on B.S. II:1.22.

INDEX